NEW YORK AND NEW JERSEY
COASTAL ADVENTURES

NEW YORK
AND
NEW JERSEY
COASTAL ADVENTURES

Whales, Beaches, Packets, Tugs, Tall Ships, Lighthouses, and More

by Betsy Frawley Haggerty

Illustrated by Dale Ingrid Swensson

A Guide Book from Country Roads Press

New York and New Jersey Coastal Adventures

Published by Country Roads Press
P.O. Box 286, Lower Main Street
Castine, Maine 04421

Text and cover design by Janet Patterson.
Illustrations by Dale Ingrid Swensson, Mount Desert, Maine.

ISBN 1-56626-097-3

Library of Congress Cataloging-in-Publication Data

Haggerty, Betsy Frawley
New York and New Jersey coastal adventures: whales, beaches, pack
ets, tugs, tall ships, lighthouses, and more / author, Betsy Frawley Haggerty: illustrator, Dale Ingrid Swensson.
p. cm.
Includes index.
ISBN 1-56626-097-3: $9.95
1. Atlantic Coast (N.Y.)—Guidebooks. 2. Atlantic Coast (N.J.)—
Guidebooks. 3. Boats and boating—New York (State)—Guidebooks.
4. Boats and boating—New Jersey—Guidebooks. I. Title.
F116.3.H34   1995
797.1'09163'46—dc20
94-45907
CIP

Printed in the United States of America.
10 9 8 7 6 5 4 3 2 1

For my parents, Betty and Jack Frawley,

with special thanks for the Turnabout

that introduced me to the sea

Acknowledgments

New York and New Jersey Coastal Adventures would never have been possible without the wisdom and moral support of my family, friends, and colleagues. Special thanks to my daughter, Kate Haggerty, and my friends, Jean Crichton and Marilee Hartley, who generously gave time to help proofread, check facts, make suggestions, and cheer me on when I needed encouragement.

Thanks also to those who took me boating, shared a canoe, told me sea stories, provided information or gave me a place to stay: Norman Brouwer, Russell Buckingham, Jack Burger, Cathy Drew, Frank Duffy, Judy Duffy, Tom Fox, Jim Gallagher, John Haggerty, Walter and Elinor Haggerty, Pamela Hepburn, John Krevey, Ella Lasky, Jack Leibolt, Cathy Lewis, Ann Loeding, Audrey Murray, Stan Nitzburg, Neil Osborne, Nancy O'Reilly, Jack Palmer, Jill Pincus, Jack Putnam, Jerry Roberts, Barbara Robertson, Stan Rosenzweig, Bob Stryker, Jim Wetteroth, and Tom Winslow.

Contents

Introduction

Right and left, the streets take you waterward ... Go from Corlears Hook, to Coentes Slip, and from thence by Whitehall northward. What do you see?—Posted like silent sentinels all around the town, stand thousands upon thousands of mortal men fixed in ocean reveries ... Nothing will content them but the extremist limits of the land ... They must get just as nigh the water as they possibly can without falling in.
—Herman Melville
Moby Dick

Water is one of the great magnetic forces of my life. I am drawn to it inexorably.

Growing up four blocks from the Hudson River in Troy, New York, I was a fan of "Little Toot" and loved to stand by the river and watch tugs maneuver massive barges into the locks that marked the beginning of what was then called the New York State Barge Canal. Later, I learned the magic of sailing in the ocean: the haunting sounds of gulls, the calming lap of water against a hull,

1

the thrilling power of harnessed wind, the pleasure of beaching a small boat and exploring an empty island, the fun of competing in a sailboat race, and the peace of sunset in a quiet anchorage.

As an adult, living in New York City, I have spent nearly every free moment trying to get on or near the water. This quest for waterborne adventure has led me down a number of dead-end streets and brought me in contact with more fences than I care to remember, but it has also introduced me to some wonderful people and led to some fantastic discoveries. *New York and New Jersey Coastal Adventures* is the fruit of these explorations. It is a leisure-time guide for people who love the water, and an insider's Baedeker that will lead New York's and New Jersey's visitors and residents to the best of the many maritime destinations and adventures the two states have to offer.

New York and New Jersey Coastal Adventures will bring you aboard classic tour boats, like the Circle Line's cruise around Manhattan, billed as America's favorite boat ride, and point you to off-the-beaten-track excursions, like kayak trips though Jamaica Bay. It will take you sailing, fishing, beachcombing, and whale watching. It will guide you through canal locks, up lighthouse stairs, down river rapids, along coastal roads, aboard historic ships, and out into the Atlantic in a jet-powered speedboat that travels forty miles an hour. It will also introduce you to the groups, clubs, and individuals that make up New York's and New Jersey's informal network of sailors, river lovers, and hikers who are always looking for kindred souls to help crew on their sailboats, join a canoe trip, or participate in a waterside hike.

With over 3,000 miles of coast, rivers, and canals, New York and New Jersey offer adventures at every new cove and twist in the river. I could not have included, or even discovered, them all. What I have attempted to do is paint a seascape that inspires you to explore and enjoy New York's and New Jersey's incredible opportunities for recreation on the water.

Fair winds.

◆ 1 ◆

Cruising the Coast: Schooners to Speedboats, Kayaks to the *QE2*

Fog hovered over New York Harbor. In the distance, thirty-five grand square-riggers unfurled their sails and began moving slowly toward Manhattan, ghost ships parading through the morning haze in commemoration of the 500th Anniversary of Christopher Columbus's voyage to America. It was a magnificent sight, but one that distressed me.

I had been invited to sail aboard *Eagle,* the three-masted, 295-foot U.S Coast Guard bark that was leading this Fourth of July Parade of Sail, and the launch I was riding was late. By the time we pulled alongside, the ship was approaching the Statue of Liberty under full sail. "No more passengers," the crew chief said. But, as the *Eagle*'s crew lowered a Jacob's ladder so Coast Guard officers could board, the chief granted a reprieve. "Okay," he said grudgingly to the pleading guests. "Climb aboard, if you can handle this ladder."

Ladders make me nervous, even on land. To negotiate this one, I would have to step from a small pitching boat onto a swing-

3

ing rope ladder and climb twenty or so feet up the side of a moving ship. Never mind that I was trembling, I didn't hesitate for a second. Riding aboard *Eagle* in the 1992 OpSail celebration would be the ultimate boat ride, and there wasn't a chance in the world I would forfeit it on account of fear.

I tell this story to show that I am willing to overcome almost any obstacle for the sake of a good boat ride. Fortunately, it's rarely necessary, for New York and New Jersey offer scores of opportunities for wonderful boating adventures, almost none of which require acrobatics at sea.

Here you will find the world's most expensive cruise (a 102-day around-the-world voyage on the *Queen Elizabeth 2* for a top price of $152,440 per person) and its best boating bargain (round-trip on the Staten Island Ferry for fifty cents). In between, there are boats to relax on, to get wet on, to catch fish from, to dine aboard, to see sights from, and to commute on.

This chapter will lead you to boating activities that are destinations in themselves — sailing, fishing, canoe, and kayak trips, and cruises under power that have more than local interest. (Note: You will find boats listed in other chapters as well. Historic vessels that offer regular sailing opportunities are included here, but those that are open only for dockside tours appear in Chapter 2. Sightseeing excursions are described along with the destinations they explore; whale watches and nature cruises are listed in Chapter 7.)

Cruising Under Sail

Step aboard a sailboat for an afternoon's outing, and you will be transported to a different world. Powered by wind, away from the sounds and the rush of everyday life, you will be able to listen to the calls of seabirds, watch light dance on the water, and look at the shore from a different perspective. Fortunately, you don't need a friend with a yacht to experience these pleasures. Several passenger-carrying sailing vessels operate in New York and New Jersey, and sailing schools and clubs provide opportunities for hands-on participation.

New York

For a nineteenth-century sailing experience, take a ride on South Street Seaport's schooner *Pioneer*, where sails are raised and trimmed the old-fashioned way — with muscle power. (No high-speed winches here.) Passengers can join in the work, or just watch. Built in 1885 as a Delaware Bay cargo carrier, the 102-foot *Pioneer* is the only surviving American iron-hulled vessel. Until it was refurbished in the 1960s, the *Pioneer* worked out of East Coast ports hauling coal, lumber, brick, and eventually oil. Now this sturdy, graceful vessel carries passengers past the Statue of Liberty and the skyscrapers of Lower Manhattan during daily ninety-minute and two-hour cruises. Season: May through September. Prices: $12 to $16; children, seniors, students, and museum members less.

The *Pioneer* also has a free, well-organized sail-training program. Volunteers, who must spend twelve or more hours a month working on the boat, learn seamanship skills and assist the professional crew during passenger sails. For those who live in the area, it's a fantastic way to be part of a sailing community and help the Seaport continue a sailing tradition. No sailing experience is necessary, but crew spots are limited and volunteers must be serious about their commitment. Volunteers are also needed for ship restoration work during the off-season.

◆ **FOR MORE INFORMATION:** *Pioneer*, Pier 16, South Street Seaport Museum, New York, NY 10038; 212-748-8786 (tickets and reservations); 212-748-8727 (volunteer sailing crew and ship restoration).

After a four-year, $1 million restoration, the ***Lettie G. Howard***, South Street Seaport's nineteenth-century fishing schooner, began its second century of sailing in 1994. Now a National Historic Landmark, the 125-foot schooner was built in Essex, Massachusetts, in 1893 and is the last surviving example of the sleek Fredonia-model schooners that sailed into New York's Fulton Fish Market at the turn of the century. In its new mission as an educational sail training vessel, the *Lettie* will be used to teach sailing skills, traditional fishing techniques, maritime history, folk arts, and marine ecology. The program, which includes both day sails in New York Harbor and week-long fishing expeditions in Long Island Sound, is open to school groups, social service programs, cultural organizations, and interested individuals. Fees vary and some scholarship assistance is available. The *Lettie* also has a training program for volunteers, similar to the *Pioneer*'s.

◆ **FOR MORE INFORMATION:** *Lettie G. Howard*, Pier 15, South Street Seaport Museum; 212-748-8600 or 748-8592.

When you look at the *Petrel,* a 1938-built, seventy-foot wooden yawl that offers public sails out of New York City's Battery Park, you will understand why President John F. Kennedy selected it to be his presidential yacht. Designed as an ocean racer by world-famous yacht designers Sparkman & Stephens, the *Petrel* is a fast boat that shows the classic elegance of yachting's golden age. After Kennedy's death, the U.S. Coast Guard sold it at auction in 1964 to photographer and yachtsman Hans Van Nes. In 1974 Captain Nick Van Nes (Hans's son) formed a company called Bring Sailing Back, Inc., and literally brought sail touring back to New York Harbor for the first time in decades. After more than twenty years working in the harbor, the *Petrel* has become a New York City institution, offering lunch-hour, after-work, sunset, moonlight, and weekend public sails from mid-April through September. There's a cash bar onboard, and passengers are welcome to bring sandwiches or other picnic food. The price averages $10 per person, per hour. Call for schedule and reservations.

◆ **FOR MORE INFORMATION:** *Petrel,* Pier 5 Battery Park, New York, NY 10004; 212-825-1976.

The *Mary E.*, a seventy-two-foot historic schooner now carrying passengers for two-hour cruises out of Greenport, Long Island, was built in Bath, Maine, in 1906 and had a long career as a fishing vessel and World War II mail boat before being refitted for passengers in the 1960s. Owner/captain Teddy Charles operates the boat with the relaxed hand of an old salt — which he is — but if you want to hear some interesting stories, get him talking about music. Charles is an acclaimed vibraphone player and jazz composer who worked regularly with Charlie Mingus and Miles Davis. He still does occasional gigs, but since the clubs aren't what they used to be, mostly he'd rather go sailing. Season: May to October. Prices: $15 and up.

◆ **FOR MORE INFORMATION:** *Mary E.*, Preston's Dock, Greenport, NY 11796; 516-477-8966.

The HMS *Rose*, a three-masted, 179-foot square-rigger, is Long Island Sound's resident tall ship. Based in Bridgeport, Connecticut, directly across the sound from Port Jefferson on Long Island, the *Rose* is the only Class A tall ship in the United States certified as a sailing school vessel. The ship, built in 1970, is a replica of an eighteenth-century British frigate that was stationed in the Caribbean during the French and Indian War. It sails both in Long Island Sound and on ocean cruises to U.S. and foreign ports. Training sessions, which include living aboard and hands-on learning opportunities, can last anywhere from one day to a month or more, and are open to people of all ages and abilities. No prior sailing experience is necessary. Tuition, including meals and bunk accommodations, is about $100 per day.

◆ **FOR MORE INFORMATION:** HMS *Rose* Foundation, Inc., 1 Bostwick Ave., Bridgeport, CT 06605; 203-335-1433.

The Hudson River Sloop *Clearwater* (see Chapter 4) also sails out of Long Island Sound and New Jersey coastal ports.

◆ **FOR MORE INFORMATION:** Hudson River Sloop *Clearwater,* Inc., 112 Market Street, Poughkeepsie, NY 12601; 914-454-7673.

New Jersey

The schooner *Richard Robbins* is a living piece of New Jersey's maritime history. Built in 1902 and operated for fifty years as a Delaware Bay oyster dredger, the eighty-foot gaff-rigged, two-masted schooner was refitted to carry passengers in the 1960s. Since the mid-1980s, owner/captain Alan Jadro has been running cruises and charters in New York Harbor and the Hudson River. Although the bulk of his business is private parties (which start at $42 per person, twenty-eight-person minimum), Jadro also offers public sails and dinner cruises several times a month, as well as occasional overnight trips. Season: May to October. Prices: $21 to $55; more for overnights. The *Richard Robbins* sails out of Jersey City.

◆ **FOR MORE INFORMATION:** Classic Sail Windjammer Co., Inc., P.O. Box 459, Madison, NJ 07940; 201-966-1684.

The *Yankee,* a 1980s-built schooner designed along classic lines, is the only sail-powered cruise that captures the fresh breezes off New Jersey's southern coast. Sailing from Sunset Wharf between Cape May and Wildwood, the eighty-foot-long *Yankee* cruises through the Intracoastal Waterway, Cape May Harbor, and in the dolphin-rich waters of the nearby Atlantic Ocean. Passengers can join in sailing the boat, or just relax and enjoy the sights and the breeze. Season: May through October. Prices: $20 to $25 for two- and three-hour cruises; children less.

◆ **FOR MORE INFORMATION:** *Yankee,* P.O. Box 98, Cape May, NJ 08204; 609-884-1919.

The 115-foot wooden schooner *A. J. Meerwald/Clyde A. Phillips,* a relic of the heyday of the Delaware Bay oyster industry, will sail the coast again thanks to a total reconstruction and restoration by the not-for-profit Delaware Bay Schooner Project. Beginning in late 1995 or early 1996, the *Meerwald,* which was built in 1928 on New Jersey's Delaware Bay shore, will be a sailing classroom where passengers will help sail the boat and learn about the natural resources and maritime culture of the Delaware Estuary. The boat will travel along New Jersey's Delaware Bay and Atlantic Ocean shores, offering a full program of educational sails for both school and adult groups. Until then, visitors can watch the meticulously authentic restoration taking place in Bivalve, New Jersey. Volunteers are welcome to help with the ship work or to join a volunteer crew program when the *Meerwald* begins sailing again.

◆ **FOR MORE INFORMATION**: Delaware Bay Schooner Project, P.O. Box 57, Dorchester, NJ 08316; 609-785-2060.

If you need a sailing fix in the heart of winter, go to Atlantic City for **Sail Expo**, the American Sail Advancement Program's (ASAP) annual nine-day celebration of sailing, held in February at the Atlantic City Convention Center. Begun in 1993, this sailors' get-together is a mega-boat show with extensive boat and equipment exhibits. What makes it unique, however, is a program of more than 300 top-quality sailing lectures and seminars — on everything from engine maintenance to advanced racing to Caribbean chartering — plus dinners, parties, and an indoor sailing pool, where you can sail a dinghy in a fan-generated eight-knot breeze. ASAP claims it's the most fun a sailor can expect to have in February in the Northeast. And it is.

◆ **FOR MORE INFORMATION**: American Sail Advancement Program, 200 Harrison Avenue, Newport, RI; 401-841-0900.

The Sailors' Network

New York and New Jersey are among the East Coast's most active sailing areas, with more than 150 yacht clubs, plus countless sailing groups, community sailing programs, and sailing schools. Almost all offer opportunities for people who are looking to be more than passengers on an afternoon cruise.

Since skippers, particularly those who race their boats, regularly need crew, experienced sailors and even enthusiastic beginners can often trade their skills (from cooking to trimming sheets) for sailing time. All it takes is dedicated networking, a firm commitment to be there when the skipper needs you, and a willingness to help on the boat. In most sailing communities, both formal organizations and informal meeting places provide the link between crewless boats and boatless crew-people. The following are potential sailing connections.

Sailing Courses and Community Programs

The American Red Cross, the U.S. Power Squadron, the U.S. Coast Guard Auxiliary, and dozens of community and privately operated sailing schools in New York and New Jersey give both classroom and on-the-water sailing courses. Prices range from free to several hundred dollars. Several schools run clubs where you can keep sailing after you learn the basics, and both instructors and other students are great sources of information about sailing events and organizations.

For example, one of the best sailors' networks in metropolitan New York/New Jersey grew out of a Thursday night sailing class at the American Red Cross building in Manhattan. The teacher, Tom Winslow, a professional captain who virtually gave up his law practice to sail, lectures about sailing with the passion and charisma of an old-time preacher. He then hosts an informal après-class get-together at a local watering hole that draws sailors from all over the area. Insider's tip: If you are in Manhattan on a Thursday night, stop at Donohue's Bar, West 72nd Street and Broadway, between 9:00 and 10:00 p.m. There's a good chance you'll find Winslow and his fellow sailors there.

The United States Sailing Association publishes a "Community Sailing Directory" that lists community programs, sailing associations, and commercially operated sailing schools in all fifty states. This excellent resource includes more than fifty sailing schools and associations in New York and twenty in New Jersey. First published in 1994, the directory is free and scheduled for yearly updates.

◆ **FOR MORE INFORMATION:**

Tom Winslow's Red Cross Sailing Course, 212-595-1271.

Community Sailing Council, United States Sailing Association, Box 209, Goat Island Marina, Newport, RI 02840; 401-849-5200.

Sailing Organizations

Created twenty-five years ago as a place where skippers could find crew and vice versa, the **New York Sailing Club** now has more than 125 members from New York and New Jersey, about half of whom own boats. Monthly lectures and meetings, open to the public, are held in Manhattan. Newcomers are always welcome. The New York Sailing Club is typical of a number of local organizations in New York and New Jersey formed for the specific purpose of bringing sailors together. Most list their meetings in local newspapers.

Other clubs, specifically for single sailors, sponsor parties and sailing events. One of the most active of these is the fifteen-year-old **Sound Sailing Club**, which has about a hundred members in New York and New Jersey. The club takes credit for bringing hundreds of sailing crews together and introducing dozens of now-married couples. Outdoors organizations, such as the Appalachian Mountain Club and the Sebago Canoe Club, also have sailing programs geared to non-boat-owners.

◆ **FOR MORE INFORMATION:**
New York Sailing Club, 212-580-2136.
Sound Sailing Club, P.O. Box 1307, Ansonia Station, New York, NY 10023; 212-595-1271.
Long Island Single Sailors Association, 516-756-1010.
Appalachian Mountain Club, 202 East 39th Street, New York, NY 10016; 212-986-1430.
Sebago Canoe Club, Paerdegat Basin, Foot of Avenue N, Brooklyn, NY 11236; 717-241-3683.

Yacht Racing Associations

Local yacht racing associations, which sponsor seminars, lectures, and races, will provide information on events and give you contacts at yacht clubs where racing skippers may be looking for crew. The United States Sailing Association, the national governing body for the sport of sailing, also can provide information and names of people to contact at the seven New York and New Jersey associations.

◆ **FOR MORE INFORMATION:** United States Sailing Association, Box 209, Goat Island Marina, Newport, RI 02840; 401-849-5200.

Cruising Under Power

Robert Fulton triggered America's romance with steam- and power-driven vessels when he launched the *Clermont* from a West Side Manhattan pier in 1807. For the next century and a half, New York and New Jersey waters were crowded with passenger-carrying ferries, excursion boats, and ocean liners. But by the mid-twentieth century, airplanes and automobiles had captured people's fancies, and for a time, water travel fell out of vogue.

In the 1980s, however, people rediscovered the magic of the sea and the pleasure of short cruises. Since then, dinner boats, small ferries, and sightseeing vessels have made a dramatic come-back in New York and New Jersey waters, giving visitors the chance to enjoy a water's-eye view of almost every coastal town and riverfront area. The following are unusual, offbeat, or long-distance cruises that merit special attention (local dinner and sightseeing excursions are listed by region in other chapters).

Speedboats

In Atlantic City, where everything is hype and glitz, you might be skeptical of the term "thrill ride" to describe *Miss Atlantic City*, a forty-passenger, jet-powered open boat. But after five minutes of speeding along at forty miles an hour and skidding around *S* turns in the Intracoastal Waterway, you will know that, this time at least, they are telling the truth. The one-hour ride is exhilarating without being scary, fun for kids, and particularly pleasing to the over-forty crowd who remember the days when speedboats were a big Jersey Shore attraction. (I heard shrieks and giggles of glee from the World War II veterans and their wives who sat behind me.)

To almost everyone's delight, speedboat cruises have come back to the Jersey Shore. The original *Miss Atlantic City* — "the world's biggest, fastest, most beautiful speedboat" — was a converted PT boat that zipped up and down the coast in the 1950s, along with the *Flying Saucer, Flying Cloud,* and *Flying Pony,* which operated out of Ocean City. For one reason or another they all disappeared, and a tradition died until the early 1990s, when *Shore Shot,* the first of this new generation of speedboats, began operating out of Cape May.

These new oceangoing boats — there were five operating by 1994 — are all variations on a theme. They are large (the biggest carries over a hundred passengers), they are fast (up to 50 mph), they are wet, and they are fun. One-hour to ninety-minute boat rides include both slow-speed harbor sightseeing and wave-piercing ocean thrills. The boats operate from Memorial Day until mid-October, weather permitting, and rides cost between $10 and $20 depending on the length of the cruise.

The Shore Shot *out of Cape May*

◆ FOR MORE INFORMATION:

Miss Atlantic City, Farley State Marina, Atlantic City. Mailing address: P.O. Box 20, Absecon, NJ 08201; 609-348-0800.

Flying Saucer, Ocean City Marina, Third and Bay Streets, Ocean City, NJ 08226; 609-399-5011.

Silver Bullet, Wildwood Marina, 508 West Rio Grande Avenue, Wildwood, NJ 08260; 609-522-6060.

PT-109, Sinn's Dock, 6006 Park Boulevard, Wildwood Crest, NJ, 08260; 609-522-3934.

Shore Shot, Miss Chris Fishing Center, Third Avenue and Wilson Drive, Cape May, NJ 08204; 609-886-6161.

Specialty Cruises

If you've always wanted to ride on a tugboat, you can make that dream a reality in New York Harbor. The *W. O. Decker,* a small working tug owned by New York City's South Street Seaport Museum, is available for tours. Built in 1930, this diesel-powered wooden tug worked as a towboat in New York, New Jersey, and Connecticut for more than four decades. Now fully restored, it offers charter cruises through the working waterfront for groups of up to six people for $150 per hour.

◆ **FOR MORE INFORMATION:** *W. O. Decker,* South Street Seaport Museum, New York, NY 10038; 212-748-8786.

Would you like to sail on a tall ship, travel eighty miles offshore to watch New Jersey's scallop fleet at work, or study the skeletons of classic steam and ferry boats as you cruise by New York Harbor's incredible ship graveyard? The most interesting boat trips in New York and New Jersey are often special outings sponsored by not-for-profit groups such as the National Maritime Historical Society, the American Littoral Society, the Steamship Historical Society, and the World Ship Society, which ran the above-listed excursions. Many such cruises are annual events open to nonmembers on a space-available basis. To get schedule information, contact the historic or environmental organizations listed in Chapters 2 and 7, and ask to be put on their mailing lists.

NY/NJ specialty cruises are diverse enough to suit almost every imaginable interest, but there is one you should avoid. "People die to get on it, but we don't get a lot of repeat business," jokes one of the operators of the **Hart Island Ferry**. The ferry is run by the New York City Department of Transportation as a floating hearse that carries unclaimed bodies in coffins of white pine for burial in New York City's Potter's Field. The half-mile trip between City Island in the Bronx and Hart Island in Long Island Sound is not open to the public.

Large Cruise Ships

New York Harbor has been port to the world's greatest ships since the 1830s when the Cunard, French, and Italian lines began sailing across the Atlantic to Manhattan's North River piers. Although the heyday of ocean travel ended in 1958 with the start of commercial jet service to Europe, you can still hear the low blast of ships' horns and watch stately cruise ships going in and out of the harbor on weekends from April through October. Over 200 passenger voyages head out annually, carrying upward of 400,000 people, according to the Port Authority of NY and NJ.

In warm-weather months, several cruise lines regularly operate out of New York, taking weekly voyages to Bermuda, Canada, the Caribbean, and short cruises to nowhere, as well as occasional transatlantic crossings and luxurious around-the world cruises. The least expensive ocean adventure is a two-day party cruise (offered by several lines), which starts at about $500 per person, for a voyage along the Long Island or New Jersey coasts, just far enough offshore to feel the gentle ocean roll and experience the fun of shipboard living — plentiful food and drink, Broadway- and Las Vegas-style entertainment, casino gambling, organized games, sun, swimming, and peaceful ocean views.

The best way to book any cruise is through a travel agent, since prices vary and many discounts are available. However, the cruise lines are happy to send brochures and, in some cases, preview videos. The following maintain a regular schedule of cruises sailing from New York.

Carnival Cruise Line
3655 NW 8th Avenue
Miami, FL 33178
305-599-2600

Celebrity Cruises
5200 Blue Lagoon Drive
Miami, FL 33126
800-437-3111

Cunard Line Ltd.
555 Fifth Avenue
New York, NY 10017
800-221-4770

Norwegian Cruise Line
95 Merrick Way
Coral Gables, FL 33134
305-447-9669

Regal Cruise Line
69 Spring Street
Ramsey, NJ 07446
201-934-3753

Regency Cruises
260 Madison Avenue
New York, NY 10016
800-734-3629

Royal Caribbean Cruises, Ltd.
1050 Caribbean Way
Miami, FL 33132
800-327-6700

Small Cruise Ships

The **Clipper Cruise Line** sails 100-passenger ships to waterways and destinations known for their natural beauty or cultural interest. The *Nantucket Clipper* departs from several East Coast ports and visits New York during art cruises and fall foliage tours. The company prides itself on its culturally sophisticated, but casual, cruising atmosphere, typified by expert lectures rather than "corny" (their word) entertainment. The pace is slow and attracts passengers who prefer a quiet, intimate style of cruising. Prices start at $1,100 per person, with the average in the $3,000 to $4,000 range.

◆ **FOR MORE INFORMATION:** Clipper Cruise Line, 7711 Bonhomme Avenue, St. Louis, MO 63105; 800-325-0010 or 314-727-2929.

The **American/Canadian/Caribbean Line** also offers comfortable, casual small-ship cruises of the Erie Canal in the summer (see Chapter 6) and southern ports in the winter. Although New York Harbor and New Jersey are not themselves destinations, the ships travel through Long Island Sound and New Jersey's coastal waters on their way to other locations, passing the Statue of Liberty and other landmarks along the way.

◆ **FOR MORE INFORMATION:** American/Canadian/Caribbean Line, Inc., P.O. Box 368, Warren, RI 02885; 800-556-7450 or 401-247-0995.

Fishing the Deep

"Bluefish." "Fluke." "Cod." "Tuna." Bold-lettered signs beckon would-be anglers to the docks in seacoast towns, offering a dazzling menu of fishing opportunities on more than 500 party and charter boats that sail offshore and in the bays of New York and New Jersey. Many world fishing records have been set in these waters, which, some say, are the richest fishing grounds on the East Coast.

Boats with names like *Duke O' Fluke, Flounder Pounder, Sea Raider,* and *Adventurer* sail virtually every day from early spring through late fall (some even have winter schedules) and require no advance reservations. For as little as $20 a half day, you get bait, tackle, plenty of free advice, and the chance to battle an eighteen-pound bluefish or bring home a pail of flounder — a nice change of pace if your home waters happen to be lakes and streams.

Head boats, as these open boats are called because they charge on a per-head basis, used to be no-frills operations that catered to a die-hard, mostly male crowd of fishermen. Now, many actively seek family groups and advertise sundecks, special "ladies accommodations," and reduced rates for children.

Choosing a boat is more a matter of subjective preference than a science. You will find Coast Guard–certified, seaworthy boats, fitted with the most sophisticated fish-finding equipment, sailing from dozens of New York and New Jersey ports. Among the most popular departure points are Babylon, Captree Basin, City Island, Freeport, Greenport, Montauk, Orient Point, and Sheepshead Bay in New York, and the New Jersey towns of Atlantic City, Atlantic Highlands, Barnegat Light, Belmar, Brielle, Cape May, Fortescue, Highlands, Point Pleasant, Sea Isle City, and Wildwood.

Once you decide on a location, the type of fish you want to catch, the time of day or night you want to sail, and whether you prefer a bay or an offshore outing, the best way to choose a boat is to walk along the dock in the late afternoon when most of the boats come in. Look at the boats and the faces of the fishermen. Listen to the conversations about fish lost and fish caught. Watch the mates as they clean and fillet the fish. Ask questions and then go with your instinct. It's probably hard to make a bad choice.

Since most fishing-boat captains are in more or less friendly competition with one another, centralized booking locations are the exception rather than the rule, but local newspapers, chambers of commerce, and bait-and-tackle shops often have listings. In addition, the following resources have information about fishing boats in their area.

Long Island

Captree Boat Basin: 516-669-6464.
Freeport Charter Boat Information: 516-378-4838.
Montauk Charter Boat Information: 516-668-2117.

New Jersey

Atlantic County Charter and Party Boat Association: 609-823-8515.
Atlantic Highlands Bait and Tackle Shop: 908-291-4500.
Belmar Marina: 908-681-2266.
Brielle Marine Basin: 908-528-6200.
Cape May County Party and Charter Boat Association: 609-465-2871.

Fortescue Captains and Boat Owners Association: 609-447-5115.

Southern Ocean County Chamber of Commerce: 800-292-6372.

Rowing and Paddling

New York Harbor

"Recreational rowing started in New York Harbor," says Michael K. Davis, an archaeologist and the founder of Floating the Apple, one of a number of not-for-profit groups that launched a campaign in the early 1990s to bring small hand-powered boats back to New York Harbor. I can't vouch for the historical accuracy of Davis's statement, but human-powered boats are definitely making a comeback thanks to groups like Floating the Apple and the philosophical (if not financial) support of government and park development agencies, which now assist in creating boat ramps and public access areas. Most of the boaters belong to local grassroots organizations with informal programs and they almost always welcome the involvement of kindred spirits.

◆ **FOR MORE INFORMATION:**

The Downtown Boat Club (212-966-1852) expects to have a public boathouse and kayak-launching area on a Hudson River pier by 1995.

Floating the Apple (400 West 43rd Street, 32R, New York, NY 10036; 212-564-5412) builds rowing gigs in a mid-Manhattan storefront and runs a program for their use in the Hudson River and New York Harbor.

The Hudson River Park Conservancy (141 Fifth Avenue, New York, NY 10010; 212-353-0366) is a city-state agency that is planning and building a four-mile park, with water access areas, along the West Side waterfront.

The Nubia Sculling Crew (212-477-5944) uses a thirty-four-foot canopied pseudo-Egyptian rowboat for outings and introductory classes in sculling (sliding seat rowing) in the Hudson River.

Project Sail, Inc. (23 Gramercy Park South, New York, NY 10003; 212-439-8084) is a highly regarded and long-established youth rowing and maritime education program that sponsors races and public rowing events for people of all ages.

Bays, Rivers, and Streams

If dodging tugs, barges, and ferryboats is not your idea of sport, New York and New Jersey have literally thousands of miles of quiet bays, rivers, streams, and wildlife areas that are ideal for exploring by canoe, kayak, and rowboat. Particularly popular areas include the Jamaica Bay Wildlife Area in Gateway National Park, where you can see Manhattan's skyscrapers in the distant haze as you paddle among towering reeds, and the New Jersey Pine Barrens, where you are apt to find rare orchids, beavers, eagles, osprey, and cranberry bogs. Several private outfitters, as well as not-for-profit canoe clubs, run trips and provide instruction.

◆ FOR MORE INFORMATION:

The American Littoral Society (Sandy Hook, Highlands, NJ 07732; 908-291-0055) leads trips through New Jersey's Pine Barrens and Long Island's Peconic River.

The New York/North Jersey Chapter of the Appalachian Mountain Club (202 East 39th Street, New York, NY 10016; 212-986-1430) rents canoes at a modest cost and leads both recreational and instructional trips in a number of different locations in the two states.

Sebago Canoe Club (Paerdegat Basin, Foot of Avenue N, Brooklyn, NY 11236; 717-241-3683) sponsors an extensive program of trips and courses in canoeing, kayaking, and sailing in cooperation with the American Red Cross and the American Canoe Association.

The State of New Jersey publishes an outdoor guide that lists canoe clubs and rental companies in the state. Call 800-

JERSEY-7 for a free copy. National Park Service offices at Gateway National Park (718-318-4340) and New Jersey Coastal Heritage Trail Project (609-725-0676) can also suggest canoeing locations and rental companies.

◆ 2 ◆
History Afloat: Maritime Museums and Historic Ships

The docks along New York City's South Street groaned as waves from a passing boat rolled toward shore. Wayward halyards slapped against wooden masts. A guitar played in the distance, and the voices of sailors singing sea chanteys rose up from a schooner at the end of a pier.

That's how it was a hundred years ago along the Lower Manhattan waterfront they called the Street of Ships. And that's how it is again every September when the South Street Seaport Museum sponsors the Mayor's Cup race and rendezvous for schooners and classic yachts. Dozens of captains bring their historic boats to this event — and others like it — to demonstrate the stamina and integrity of their vessels and to spend a weekend with others who share their dedication to continuing centuries-old seafaring traditions.

With ship restorations, exhibits, educational programs, and festivals, maritime museums not only portray the history of ships and mariners, but they also keep maritime culture alive by inspiring new generations to become involved in hands-on boatbuilding, ship maintenance, fishing, ecology, and sailing. Each museum, indeed every ship that is saved and restored, is the product of the passion and perseverance of individuals who dedicate themselves to preserving and promoting the heritage of the sea. This deep commitment is reflected in the variety and excellence of museum programs and exhibits in New York and New Jersey.

At these museums, visitors have the opportunity to stand on the deck of a square-rigger and imagine themselves climbing aloft in a gale and tying down a sail, or they can sit in the crew quarters of a submarine and ponder what it might be like to live under the sea for months on end. They can read whalers' logs, pick up baymen's tools, take courses in knot tying or shipbuilding, or just look at paintings and watch films. All levels of involvement are possible, from a casual browse through a collection to signing on as a full-time volunteer.

This chapter describes New York and New Jersey maritime museums and dockside ship exhibits. Historic vessels that offer public sailing programs are included in Chapter 1. Lighthouses are listed by location in other chapters. Since museum exhibits are subject to change, it is advisable to call in advance for program and schedule information.

New York
South Street Seaport Museum

South Street Seaport Museum, founded in 1967, is a vibrant maritime center in the heart of New York City's once-bustling seafaring neighborhood. It has the country's largest fleet of historic ships (in terms of tonnage), four exhibition galleries, a maritime crafts center, a working re-creation of a nineteenth-century printshop, an off-site archaeological center, an excellent marine bookstore, and a research library with a fine collection of books, photographs, and historical documents relating to New York and general maritime history.

But when people visit the South Street Seaport neighborhood in Lower Manhattan, the question they invariably ask is "Where's the museum?" The South Street Seaport Marketplace, with its boutiques, restaurants, pubs, street performers, concert stage, and three-story Pier 17 mall, dominates the area.

"We are a museum without walls," South Street president Peter Neill explains, pointing to historic ships along the piers and describing exhibits located in early-nineteenth-century buildings throughout an eleven-square-block historic district near the Brooklyn Bridge. But he and others at South Street are aware that the commercial enterprises, established to help generate funds for historic preservation, sometimes obscure the museum's work. Culture and commerce have always coexisted in this neighborhood, they say, as they double their efforts to make sure the culture gets at least equal billing. A special introductory tour, entitled "I Found the Museum," is one such attempt.

To find the historic ship collection, look for the masts at the right when you reach the pier area. Three vessels are open for dockside tours, and three are working vessels, available for passenger cruises.

The *Peking,* a 1911 German-built, steel-hulled, four-masted bark, dominates the Seaport's piers. The second largest sailing ship still in existence, the *Peking* is 347 feet long, with towering masts seventeen stories high. *Peking* carried nitrate between Europe and South America until 1931, rounding Cape Horn twice each trip, and later was used as a dormitory for a British boys school. Visitors can tour on their own, or take in special programs that include guided tours, hands-on dockside sail raisings, and a film that shows *Peking* rounding Cape Horn.

The *Wavertree,* a 293-foot, iron-hulled, three-masted square-rigger, is undergoing gradual restoration with the help of a dedicated group of volunteers. A direct descendant of the mid-nineteenth-century clipper ships, *Wavertree* was built in England in 1885 and for many years was the sailing equivalent of a tramp steamer carrying cargo between ports in Australia, South America, Europe, Africa, and the United States. Dismasted in 1911 off Cape

Horn, the ship ended its seafaring days as a sand barge in Argentina. Part of South Street Seaport's collection since 1970, the *Wavertree* is open for once-daily guided tours of the ongoing restoration.

The steel-hulled *Ambrose Lightship* was built in 1908 to stand at the entrance of the Port of New York, its lights guiding ships to the channel. *Ambrose* remained at that post until 1932, later serving as a relief lightship, and finally, near Sandy Hook, New Jersey, as Scotland Light. Donated to the museum by the U.S. Coast Guard in 1968, *Ambrose* now houses a permanent exhibit on the history and technology of navigation, from sextants to satellites.

Be sure to visit the South Street Seaport Museum at the foot of Manhattan

The Seaport's three working vessels — the schooners *Pioneer* and *Lettie G. Howard* and the tugboat *W. O. Decker* — are described in Chapter 1. Harbor cruises on the *Pioneer,* offered daily from May through September, enrich the Seaport experience. The Seaport Liberty Line also takes passengers on short sightseeing cruises from the museum's piers (see Chapter 3).

In addition to opening its ships for viewing, South Street Seaport organizes special exhibits and programs that make it the site of a lively and ever-changing maritime festival. These include gallery exhibits, Fulton Fish Market tours, walking tours of the historic seaport neighborhood, maritime craft workshops, marine art symposiums, hands-on programs for children and families, sail training, boat shows, regattas, and waterfront festivals.

An often-missed but particularly wonderful place to visit at South Street Seaport is the Maritime Crafts Center, located in a double-sized cargo container near the entrance of the piers. Here, a scrimshander, a woodcarver, and a model maker work daily at age-old sailors' crafts. Their work is gorgeous (yes, they do accept special orders) and they are happy to answer questions or simply let you watch. The three are part a community of staff members and volunteers whose dedication and skills in sailing, ship maintenance, historic preservation, and maritime crafts give the museum its soul. If you live in the area, and your interest goes beyond an occasional visit, call 212-748-8727 to find out about becoming a volunteer.

South Street Seaport Museum is open seven days a week 10:00 a.m. until 5:00 p.m. Stop first at the visitors center, 12 Fulton Street, for tickets, information, and a detailed map that will help you find the museum's many treasures. Admission: $5 for adults; less for seniors, students, and children.

◆ **FOR MORE INFORMATION:** South Street Seaport Museum, 207 Front Street, New York, NY 10038; 212-748-8600.

Intrepid Sea•Air•Space Museum

Since its opening in 1982, the Intrepid Sea•Air•Space Museum, has grown, ship-by-ship, plane-by-plane, into the world's largest naval/maritime museum. The aircraft carrier USS *Intrepid,* a

40,000-ton, 900-foot-long battle-scarred veteran of World War II and the Vietnam War, houses galleries and exhibits that highlight significant elements of twentieth-century sea, air, and space technology. A featured permanent exhibit, Undersea Frontier, contains artifacts of a number of East Coast shipwrecks, and a simulator gives the sensation of flying. Over forty aircraft, ranging from a 1910 Curtis Pusher to the CIA's Lockheed A-12 Blackbird, the fastest, highest-flying airplane ever built, line the flight deck and hanger bay.

Several other vessels are also open for tours, including:

USS *Growler,* the only strategic-missile submarine open to the public anywhere in the world. The entire 317-foot vessel, including the once top-secret missile command center, is open for exploration (to those over six years old).

USS *Edson,* a 4,000-ton, 418-foot destroyer that did combat duty off the Vietnamese coast. Tours include the weather deck,

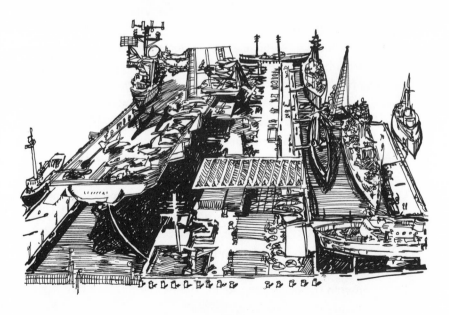

The USS Intrepid, *veteran of World War II and Vietnam, stars at the Sea•Air•Space Museum at Pier 86 in Manhattan*

bridge, officer and crew quarters, the gun-mount control room, and the engine room.

The *Nantucket* Lightship, the largest and sturdiest lightship ever built, and one of the few still capable of routine underway operation. Tours include visits to the bridge, outer decks, and crew quarters.

The Intrepid Seafest, held on weekends throughout the summer, draws police, fire, and other unusual boats to the pier for public visiting. Harbor tugs race and engage in nose-to-nose pushing contests during the annual Intrepid Tugboat Challenge, held in September.

Open year-round, seven days a week during the summer, Wednesday through Sunday the remainder of the year. Admission: $7; children under twelve, $4.

◆ **FOR MORE INFORMATION:** Intrepid Museum, Pier 86, West 46th Street and 12th Avenue, New York, NY 10036; 212-245-0072 or 212-245-2533.

Snug Harbor Cultural Center

The John A. Noble Collection, located in Staten Island at the Snug Harbor Cultural Center, celebrates the work of John A. Noble, a maritime painter, lithographer, photographer, writer, and seafarer whose images of old schooners, tugs, and wharf scenes capture the grit and drama of the working waterfront. The Noble Collection's home, an 1844-built former seamen's dormitory, is being restored as a maritime art and study center that will house a library, galleries, a printmaking studio, and education programs. Visitors are invited to view the work in progress, Monday through Friday from 9:00 a.m. to 2:00 p.m., and by appointment.

From 1831 until 1976, the eighty-acre, twenty-eight-building Sailor's Snug Harbor was a home for retired seafarers. Now a major Staten Island cultural center, Snug Harbor also houses a children's museum, a botanical museum, and performing arts facilities. Free weekend tours are offered.

Travelers' tip: For a good view of the waterfront scene that inspired Noble, stop at R. H. Tugs, a casual publike restaurant less than a quarter of a mile away. Tugs has large picture windows and an outdoor deck that overlooks the Kill Van Kull, the harbor's busiest and narrowest shipping channel. Container ships and tankers pass by so closely that you can often hear crew members talking. Snug Harbor and R. H. Tugs are easily reached via the Staten Island Ferry and a public bus that travels along Richmond Terrace.

◆ **FOR MORE INFORMATION:**

John A. Noble Collection/Snug Harbor Cultural Center, 1000 Richmond Terrace, Staten Island, NY 10301; 718-447-6490 (Noble Collection), 718-448-2500 (Snug Harbor).

R. H. Tugs, 1115 Richmond Terrace, Staten Island, NY 10301; 718-447-6369.

Maritime Industry Museum at Fort Schuyler

Housed within the walls of a nineteenth-century fort built to defend the East River entrance to New York City, the Maritime Industry Museum is part of the State University of New York (SUNY) Maritime College, America's oldest maritime educational institution. Its collection of artifacts, dioramas, models, nautical photos, and prints traces the evolution of seafaring from the Phoenicians to the present. Highlights are a replica model of the Brooklyn Navy Yard during World War II; a pictorial overview of the Port of New York, with a scale model of the Port Newark/Port Elizabeth Terminal; and a set of exquisite ship models. Most items in the ever-growing collection have been donated by representatives of the maritime industry and include memorabilia from prominent, but now-defunct, shipping companies and decommissioned ships.

SUNY Maritime College has been located at Fort Schuyler since 1938 and welcomes visitors to its parklike campus overlooking western Long Island Sound near the Bronx end of the Throgs Neck Bridge. When schedules permit, the college's 565-foot training ship, *Empire State VI*, is open for tours. Arrangements should be made in advance.

The museum is open year-round, Monday through Friday, 9:00 a.m. to 4:00 p.m., plus weekends from September to May,

Saturdays, 9:00 a.m. to 4:00 p.m., Sundays 12:00 p.m. to 4:00 p.m. Closed holidays. Free admission.

◆ **FOR MORE INFORMATION:** Maritime Industry Museum, SUNY Maritime College at Fort Schuyler, 6 Pennyfield Avenue, Bronx, NY 10465; 718-409-7218 (museum), 718-409-7200 (ship visits).

American Merchant Marine Museum

"Ships made America," the American Merchant Marine Museum proclaims in its brochure. And the museum (located on the Kings Point, Long Island campus of the U.S. Merchant Marine Academy in the town of Great Neck about twenty miles from Manhattan) illustrates the point with artfully displayed ship models, artwork, and nautical memorabilia that emphasize the important role merchant mariners have played in American history. Exhibits include a collection of rare navigational instruments; a gallery devoted to the tugboat industry; fifty ship models, including an eighteen-foot model of the passenger ship SS *Washington;* a century-old steam engine restored to working condition; and marine paintings and photographs. One gallery depicts the contributions of the merchant marine during wartime; another houses the National Maritime Hall of Fame, a permanent exhibit that honors great people and great ships in maritime history.

The academy, a tuition-free United States training college in the tradition of West Point and the U.S. Naval Academy, educates young men and women for careers in the merchant marine. The campus, located in the former Gold Coast estate of automobile magnate Walter P. Chrysler, has expansive views of Long Island Sound, as well as an interesting fleet of training ships and racing sailboats that can be seen along the docks. The academy is open to the public daily from 9:00 a.m. to 5:00 p.m. The museum is open eleven months a year on Tuesday and Wednesday, 11:00 a.m. to 3:00 p.m., and on Saturday and Sunday, 1:00 to 4:30 p.m. Closed during July. Free admission.

◆ **FOR MORE INFORMATION:** American Merchant Marine Museum, U.S. Merchant Marine Academy, Kings Point, NY 11024; 516-773-5515.

Cold Spring Harbor Whaling Museum

Founded in 1936 and located on Long Island's north shore about thirty miles from Manhattan, the Cold Spring Harbor Whaling Museum has over 6,000 artifacts that recall the village's days as a maritime center and whaling port. The star attraction is a fully equipped, thirty-foot whaleboat, used in 1912–1913 on the last voyage of the Long Island–built whaling brig *Daisy*. In addition, the museum displays encompass a 700-piece scrimshaw collection, marine paintings, ship models, whaling implements, and films of whales and whaling, as well as a hands-on marine mammal bone display. The museum also sponsors educational programs and special events, including walking tours that highlight Cold Spring Harbor's whaling past. "Bedlam Street," as Main Street was called when whalemen used it for the site of their boisterous post-voyage celebrations, is a favorite stop. Open year-round, 11:00 a.m. to 5:00 p.m., Tuesday through Sunday (except Thanksgiving, Christmas, and New Year's Day). Admission: $2; seniors and children less.

♦ **FOR MORE INFORMATION:** Cold Spring Harbor Whaling Museum, P.O. Box 25, Main Street, Cold Spring Harbor, NY 11724; 516-367-3418.

East End Seaport Maritime Museum

An infant with great promise, the East End Seaport Maritime Museum is located in Greenport, Long Island. In just four years, its founders — a group of local marine enthusiasts organized as the not-for-profit East End Seaport and Marine Foundation — have completely rebuilt a historic lighthouse, instituted a highly successful annual maritime festival, and created a museum in a former railway station.

The museum, which first opened in August 1993, is a work in progress, but its exhibits already include a replicated bow section of the first ship built in Greenport, the original lens and clockworks from the Plum Island Lighthouse, and photos, models, and documents illustrating such topics as lighthouse restoration, yacht racing, shipbuilding, fishing, and Greenport's famed Picket Patrol — a group of sailors, also called the Hooligan Navy, who used wooden yachts to patrol the coast during World War II under the direction of the U.S. Navy and Coast Guard. A sea-life exhibit with three large tanks containing live finfish and shellfish from local waters opened in 1994. Open Friday, Saturday, and Sunday afternoons during summer, and by appointment. Small admission charge.

The group's first undertaking was the reconstruction of Long Beach Bar Light, known locally as "Bug Light" because its construction on tall piles made it look like a gigantic water bug. The original light, built in 1870, burned to the ground in 1963. In 1990, the East End group raised funds, built a replica house in sections in a Greenport shipyard, then floated it on a barge to the original lighthouse site, and raised it into place. The U.S. Coast Guard has since reactivated it as an aid to navigation. The light, which is situated on a sand bar in Orient Harbor about two miles east of Greenport, is accessible by boat only, and open to the public only during special festivals and tours.

◆ **FOR MORE INFORMATION:** East End Seaport and Marine Foundation, One Bootleg Alley, P.O. Box 624, Greenport, NY 11944; 516-477-0004.

Regina Maris

A 139-foot, three-masted barkentine, built of white oak nearly ninety years ago, the *Regina Maris* has had many lives — cargo vessel, grain hulk, private yacht, passenger ship, research vessel, sunken ship, and, now, dockside attraction.

In 1991, a group of maritime preservationists, working in conjunction with the National Maritime Historical Society, brought the badly deteriorated *Regina Maris* to Greenport. They immediately began an effort to stabilize the ship and raise funds for its restoration as a research and sea education vessel. Volunteers work regularly on the slow restoration while the ship is docked and open for public visits in Greenport. As soon as funding is available, *Regina Maris* will be dry-docked for total renovation.

For a view of life aboard the *Regina Maris* during an Arctic research cruise, read the late Harvey Oxenhorn's wonderful memoir, *Tuning the Rig* (Harper and Row, 1990).

♦ **FOR MORE INFORMATION:** Save the Regina Maris, Ltd., P.O. Box 645, Greenport, NY 11944; 516-477-2121.

The three-masted barkentine Regina Maris, *Greenport, Long Island*

Sag Harbor Whaling and Historical Museum

The whaling industry in Sag Harbor reached its peak in 1845, the year that shipowner Benjamin Huntting built a three-story Greek Revival mansion in the center of town. Now home of the Sag Harbor Whaling and Historical Museum, Huntting's mansion — which says "Masonic Temple" in large letters on the front — conveys the culture and customs that evolved during whaling days. (The Masonic Temple and the Order of the Eastern Star occupy the building's second and third floors, and the first time I saw the sign I figured I was in the wrong place.)

But, on second glance, I noticed the wire sculpture of a whaleboat on the front lawn and saw the small whaling museum sign. The outdoor display also includes a life-size replica of a whaleboat from the ship *Concordia,* which first sailed from Sag Harbor in 1837, and three kettles, called try-works, which were used to boil blubber down for whale oil.

The jawbones of a right whale frame the entranceway and lead visitors to exhibits that emphasize whaling-era lifestyles, rather than actual seafaring. Nineteenth-century paintings, china, needlework, children's toys and games, a gun collection, and kitchen utensils occupy several rooms. The mansion's grand staircase, a stained-glass skylight, and the marble fireplace in the formal parlor evoke the elegance of a prosperous shipowner's home.

A collection of whalers' tools and harpoons, a display of scrimshaw done aboard ship, and mementos that whalers brought home from the sea introduce the business of whaling. The most moving exhibit is of whalers' logs, journals, and letters describing the voyages, many of which took sailors around Cape Horn to the Pacific Ocean and kept them at sea for up to four years at a time. Open mid-May until October. Small admission charge. Note: Horton Point Lighthouse, in the town of Southold on the North Fork, also displays a collection of whaling tools and memorabilia, some of which belonged to Sag Harbor whalers (see Chapter 3).

◆ **FOR MORE INFORMATION:** Sag Harbor Whaling and Historical Society, Main and Garden Streets, P.O. Box 1327, Sag Harbor, NY 11963; 516-725-0770.

East Hampton Town Marine Museum

Offshore whalers, farmer-fishermen, baymen, and deep-water fishermen have worked the waters off Long Island's East End for more than 300 years. The East Hampton Town Marine Museum, which overlooks the dunes and the Atlantic Ocean in Amagansett, depicts the struggles and triumphs of the region's long relationship with the sea. The evolution of whaling, shellfishing, and haul seining is presented in dioramas, models, and pictures. Other exhibits concern shipwrecks, lifesaving, sportfishing, and ocean ecology. Open Tuesday through Sunday, July 4 through Labor Day; weekends during June and September. Closed the remainder of the year. Small admission charge.

◆ **FOR MORE INFORMATION:** East Hampton Town Marine Museum, 101 Main Street, East Hampton, NY 11937.

Long Island Maritime Museum

At the Long Island Maritime Museum, you can go back to the late nineteenth century when Great South Bay's warm brackish waters were a rich breeding ground for world-famous Blue Point oysters. Two restored oystering vessels, the sixty-foot schooner *Priscilla* (1888) and the thirty-six-foot sloop *Modesty* (1923), lie at the museum's docks in West Sayville, across the bay from Fire Island. A restored 1907 oyster house, where baymen culled and packed gallons and gallons of prized oysters every day, houses exhibits of harvesting, cleaning, and packing tools. Knowledgeable volunteers demonstrate equipment and describe the life of the baymen. A restored bayman's cottage, moved from another part of Sayville, is also open for tours.

The 1938 hurricane ended the prosperity of the local oyster industry. The storm cut a new inlet at Fire Island and the ocean water that poured into the bay made the waters too salty to suit the oysters. But the protected bay has continued as a prosperous fishing and yachting area.

In addition to the oystering exhibits, the museum has an extensive small boat collection, an active boatbuilding shop, a library, and a large exhibit hall in a landmarked carriage house that showcases yachting photographs and memorabilia, shipwreck photographs, ship models, paintings, and a seashell collection.

The Long Island Maritime Museum sponsors summertime festivals and events, runs an education program, publishes a lively and informative quarterly newsletter, and has numerous volunteer opportunities. Open year-round, Wednesday through Sunday. Small admission charge.

◆ FOR MORE INFORMATION: Long Island Maritime Museum, P.O. Box 184, West Sayville, NY 11796; 516-854-4974.

Hudson River Maritime Museum

Founded in 1980, the Hudson River Maritime Museum, sponsors programs and exhibits that preserve and continue Hudson River maritime traditions. Each year the museum's galleries portray a major theme in Hudson River history. For example, the 1995 exhibit "Destination Catskill Mountains, 1880 to 1920" traces a typical trip of the era, via steamer, from New York City to Kingston, where travelers then boarded a train for the mountains. The museum also sponsors a series of special events throughout the season that celebrate Hudson River traditions. A shad festival, a tugboat day, and an antique and classic boat show include maritime craft displays, food, entertainment, and opportunities to explore visiting vessels, such as the Hudson River Sloop *Clearwater,* Coast Guard cutters, historic ships, and working tugs. The *Indy 7,* a former U.S. Navy liberty launch, takes visitors to the museum-maintained Rondout II Lighthouse (see Chapter 4).

The museum's vessel collection includes the 1898 steam tug *Mathilda,* a 100-year-old shad boat, and a lifeboat from the Hudson's most beloved steamboat, *Mary Powell.* The *Elise Ann Conners,* a privately owned iron-hulled tugboat, which was built in 1881 and raised from the bottom of Rondout Creek in 1993, is now tied to the museum's dock. You can watch its owners, merchant mariners Ann Loeding and Gary Matthews, restore the boat, which once worked on the Hudson and Rondout Creek.

Rondout Creek, where the museum is located, was a major

hub of river activity during the nineteenth century — the docking place for steamers that brought cargo and vacationers to the Catskills from New York City, and a busy port for barges traveling between the river and the Delaware & Hudson Canal. Today, the area is a revitalized waterfront community with antique shops, galleries, restaurants, a trolley museum, and the Kingston Urban Cultural Park visitors center.

◆ **FOR MORE INFORMATION:** Hudson River Maritime Museum, One Rondout Landing, Kingston, NY 12401; 914-338-0071. Open May through October; small admission charge.

New Jersey

Half Moon/New Netherland Museum

The *Half Moon* (Halve Maen) is a full-size replica of the ship Henry Hudson sailed in his 1609 exploration of the coasts and rivers of what is now New York, New Jersey, Delaware, and Pennsylvania. This replica, launched in 1989, is furnished with authentic reproductions of sea chests, weapons, tools, navigational instruments, and goods from the Age of Exploration.

The ship is open for at-dock tours during which guides dressed in seventeenth-century costumes describe Hudson's voyage and shipboard life. The *Half Moon* is a working vessel that travels to waterfront events. When not on tour, it is based at Liberty State Park in Jersey City. No public sailing program is offered, but volunteer crew positions are sometimes available. A small donation is requested for admission.

The ship is the first exhibit of a planned New Netherland Museum, a re-created Dutch village that will celebrate the history of Nieuw Amsterdam. Its sponsors are currently raising funds and looking for a permanent site for the village in New York or New Jersey.

◆ **FOR MORE INFORMATION:** Half Moon Visitors Center, Liberty State Park, Jersey City, NJ 07305; 201-433-5900.

Spy House Museum Complex

The seventeenth-century Whitlock-Seabrook House, the first house constructed on the Jersey Shore, was an important patriot "spy house" during the Revolutionary War. The museum, which overlooks Sandy Hook and Lower New York Harbor, depicts the area's Revolutionary War role and tells the story of the bayshore watermen who came to this North Jersey region 300 years ago. Ship models, fishing gear, and other artifacts portray Port Monmouth's fishing and shipping heritage. Limited hours; small admission fee.

◆ **FOR MORE INFORMATION:** Spy House Museum, 119 Port Monmouth Road, Port Monmouth, NJ 07758; 908-787-1807.

Toms River Seaport Museum

The shallow, fish-rich waters of Barnegat Bay inspired baymen to design and build unique shallow-draft watercraft for hunting and fishing for waterfowl, flounder, crabs, clams, and oysters. The Toms River Seaport Society was founded in 1976 "to preserve, where possible, and recreate, when necessary," the unique history of the era when schooners, catboats, and Barnegat Bay sneakboxes sailed New Jersey's coastal waters.

The museum, located in a historic carriage house, exhibits marine artifacts, including sextants and boat models, and displays a boat collection that includes garveys, traditional rowing skiffs, and several sneakboxes — flat-decked small boats designed in the nineteenth century so that baymen could lie on deck and "sneak up" on waterfowl.

The society maintains a maritime library and sponsors an extensive program of classes and seminars in navigation, marine carpentry, marlinspike seamanship, carving, and model making. Its annual July wooden boat festival celebrates Barnegat Bay traditions with a classic boat race, wooden boat displays, maritime crafts, and family activities. Open year-round, Tuesdays and Saturdays from 10:00 a.m. to 2:00 p.m., and by appointment.

◆ FOR MORE INFORMATION: Toms River Seaport Museum, Hooper Avenue and Water Street, P.O. Box 1111, Toms River, NJ 08754; 908-349-9209.

Barnegat Bay Decoy and Baymen's Museum

In 1991, a group of South Jersey sportsmen decided they "wanted to preserve Barnegat Bay traditions before they faded from old-timers' memories" so they formed a nonprofit organization, developed community support, assembled a collection, and started a museum, which is housed in a replica of a hunting shanty that they built themselves. Today, the Barnegat Bay Decoy and Baymen's Museum displays more than a hundred carved decoys, as well as a collection of antique photographs depicting life on Barnegat Bay and exhibits on hunting, fishing, clamming, oystering, decoy carving, and charterboat fishing. The organization has 1,000 members and big plans for the future.

The goal is to create a major maritime center on a sixteen-acre site on Tuckerton Creek, where historic displays will be expanded and traditional trades and crafts will be kept alive through demonstrations and workshops in boatbuilding, clamming, fishing, sailing, and other maritime and natural science skills. The group has already contracted for the purchase of the land, and fundraising is under way. The museum is open year-round, Wednesday through Sunday from 10:00 a.m. to 4:30 p.m. Donation: $2.

◆ FOR MORE INFORMATION: Barnegat Bay Decoy and Baymen's Museum, Route 9 at Tip Seaman Park, Tuckerton, NJ 08087; 609-296-8868.

Maritime Associations

From steamships, to tugboats, to ocean liners and tall ships, each vessel type has dedicated partisans who work to preserve artifacts, mount exhibits, sponsor lectures, publish newsletters and magazines, and organize special boat excursions. Although the following groups do not have public exhibit space in New York and New Jersey, they sponsor events that may interest people who love the sea.

American Sail Training Association

The American Sail Training Association (ASTA) seeks to foster opportunities for people from all walks of life to experience seafaring aboard a sailing vessel. The organization coordinates the activities of sail-training vessels in the United States and publishes a directory of programs open to the public. Members have the opportunity to spend a day on a traditional sailing vessel during ASTA's annual meeting, held each year in a different location. Membership fees start at $35 ($15 for students).

◆ **FOR MORE INFORMATION:** ASTA, P.O. Box 1459, Newport, RI 02840; 401-864-1775.

National Maritime Historical Society

The National Maritime Historical Society (NMHS), headquartered on the east bank of the Hudson River in Peekskill, New York, is a membership organization that seeks to promote seafaring knowledge and an appreciation of the "attitudes, discipline, and sense of adventure" embodied in maritime history. The society takes an active role in ship preservation efforts, publishes *Sea History* magazine, sponsors seminars, and organizes tours and on-the-water excursions, such as an annual cruise on the tall ship HMS *Rose*. NMHS has a small gallery in Peekskill that welcomes visitors. Membership, which includes quarterly issues of *Sea History*, starts at $30 ($15 for students and retired people).

◆ **FOR MORE INFORMATION:** National Maritime Historical Society, 5 John Walsh Boulevard, P.O. Box 68, Peekskill, NY 10566; 914-737-7878.

Ocean Liner Museum

The Ocean Liner Museum finds, preserves, and displays memorabilia and artifacts from the age of ocean liner travel. The museum has no permanent home but mounts major exhibits in established New York galleries and sponsors gatherings, films, lectures, and members' cruises in various locations. Membership fees begin at $25.

◆ **FOR MORE INFORMATION:** Ocean Liner Museum, 730 Fifth Avenue, New York, NY 10019; 212-333-8639.

Steamship Historical Society

The 3,400-member Steamship Historical Society of America was founded in 1935 to bring together amateur and professional historians interested in the history of steam navigation. The society publishes a quarterly magazine, hosts tours and excursions, and maintains an extensive professionally staffed library at the University of Baltimore, which includes books, periodicals, and over 60,000 ship photographs. New York and New Jersey area chapters have regular meetings and excursions. Membership fees begin at $25.

◆ **FOR MORE INFORMATION:** Steamship Historical Society, 300 Ray Drive, Suite # 4, Providence, RI 02906; 401-274-0805.

Tugboat Enthusiasts Society

The Tugboat Enthusiasts Society is an informal association of people who share an interest in workboats of all kinds, with a membership comprised of both tugboat professionals and admirers. The organization publishes a newsletter that keeps track of tug history and happenings and sponsors an annual tugboat viewing cruise. The New York Chapter meets several times a year for lectures and slide shows. Membership fee: $25.

◆ **FOR MORE INFORMATION:** Tugboat Enthusiasts Society, c/o Joe DeMuccio, 308 Quince Street, Mt. Pleasant, SC 29464; 803-881-1173.

World Ship Society

The Port of New York Chapter of the World Ship Society is one of the largest branches of an international organization founded during the 1940s in Great Britain. Members share an interest in ships of all kinds — from freighters to luxury liners — and meet monthly for a slide show or lecture. The group organizes cruises and excursions to places of maritime interest. Membership fees start at $25.

◆ **FOR MORE INFORMATION:** World Ship Society, c/o Church of Sweden, 5 East 48th Street, New York, NY 10017.

♦ 3 ♦
Seacoast Destinations

*On the Northeastern coast of the United States between latitudes 40
and 41 north, two large chunks of land stand out from the coastline
like breakwaters. One is the flank of New Jersey, with its long line of
reefs; the other is Long Island in the State of New York, a splendid
boulevard, a hundred miles long of sand, marsh and grassland. These
two land masses approach each other at an angle, and very nearly meet:
they are separated by the entrance of New York Bay.*

—Jan Morris
The Great Port

Linked by the great port that belongs to both states, New York and
New Jersey are filled with coastal towns that celebrate and, to this
day, continue the seafaring traditions that shaped their history.
Walk by the shore in almost any Long Island or New Jersey village,
and you will discover a story worth remembering or an attraction
worth visiting.

As an example of the scores of noteworthy locations along these coasts, I have selected a sampling of New York and New Jersey destinations — starting with New York Harbor as the centerpiece — that are both enjoyable to visit and evocative of the New York / New Jersey maritime experience. They include islands, coastal regions, yachting centers, whaling villages, oyster towns, and locations with lighthouses, boat rides, and wonderful beaches.

The places featured in this chapter are located along the route of an imaginary cruise that departs from New York Harbor and sails through the East River into Long Island Sound. Visiting select ports along the way, it continues to eastern Long Island, around Montauk and into the Atlantic Ocean, stopping at Fire Island. It travels next to the New Jersey coast, and finally Delaware Bay. I chose the route as an organizing principle, not a cruising recommendation. Although it could be traveled by boat, all places listed are easily accessible by car, train, or ferry.

New York

New York Harbor

STATEN ISLAND FERRY

A cruise on the Staten Island Ferry is an hour's vacation at sea for fifty cents round-trip, and a superb introduction to New York Harbor's diverse activities and attractions. The nearly five-mile voyage between the southern tip of Manhattan and St. George, Staten Island, lasts just under a half hour each way, and travels past the best scenery New York Harbor has to offer.

The view of the Manhattan skyline is incomparable, particularly late in the day when the skyscrapers turn golden in the glow of the setting sun. Then, as darkness falls, they become an urban Milky Way with millions of twinkling lights. You pass close enough to the Statue of Liberty to take photos of your friends with the Great Lady standing prominently in the background.

The ferry also offers a fine platform for viewing the workings of the port. As soon as it pulls out of its Manhattan slip, it passes Governor's Island, Atlantic headquarters of the U.S. Coast Guard, and heads toward the shipping channels. In the distance, the Verrazano Narrows Bridge, one of the world's longest suspension bridges, spans the bay between Brooklyn and Staten Island. The giant cargo cranes of the container terminals are to starboard along the New Jersey coast, and most days you see tankers and container ships making their way in or out of the Kill Van Kull, the channel that leads to the main shipping terminals. In the course of a single day, thirty to forty massive ships move about the port, and dozens of petroleum and gravel barges ply the waterways, pulled by tugboats that make their home on the Kill.

Robbins Reef Light, the spark-plug-style lighthouse that's visible to starboard as the ferry approaches Staten Island, has a great story, which I pass on, courtesy of Francis J. Duffy, executive director of the Maritime Industry Museum at the New York State Maritime College and co-author (with William H. Miller) of *The New York Harbor Book* (TBW Books, 1986). Until its automation in 1965, Robbins Reef, like many of the small lights that guide mariners through the harbor, had living quarters inside. Seafarers still refer to it as "Katie's Light," in honor of its most famous resident, Katie Walker, who took over as keeper when her husband died in 1895. Mrs. Walker, less than five feet tall and just one hundred pounds, tended the light for thirty years, saving an estimated fifty people from nearby waters. But she gained special note for her daily two-mile rows across the bay, bringing her children to and from school in Staten Island.

The Staten Island Ferry runs at regular intervals twenty-four hours a day and carries twenty million passengers a year. All passengers must disembark in Staten Island to pay a fare, but there is time to get back on the same boat. If your schedule is flexible, try to seek out one of the 1960s-vintage ferryboats — *John F. Kennedy, Gov. Herbert H. Lehman,* and *American Legion.* Unlike the newer boats, these have outside bench seating and large fore and aft decks that make them more accommodating for cruising. Since these three (of a seven-boat fleet) are also the only car ferries, call and ask when the car ferries are running to get their schedule.

◆ **FOR MORE INFORMATION:** Staten Island Ferry Office, New York City Department of Transportation, Battery Maritime Building, New York, NY 10004; 718-390-5253.

EXPLORING THE PORT

Exploring the Port of New York and New Jersey, the nation's third busiest port (after Los Angeles and Long Beach), is an adventure. As is the case in many urban ports, access to parts of its more than 500 miles of waterfront is limited, but opportunities for water-related activities have been steadily growing since the mid-1980s. Several waterfront parks have been built, and more are under construction or being planned. Old piers are being adapted for public uses and new sailing schools, ferry routes, and tour and dinner boat operations have opened and flourished.

The area's best known attractions — South Street Seaport Museum, the Intrepid Sea•Air•Space Museum (both described in Chapter 2), the Statue of Liberty, and Ellis Island — belong on any water lover's must-see list. But it is also rewarding to explore some of the port's lesser-known points of interest.

Thus, I'll take you on the less traveled routes and leave it to other tour guides and the National Park Service to help you explore such incredible national monuments as Ellis Island and the Statue of Liberty.

◆ **FOR MORE INFORMATION:**

Statue of Liberty/Ellis Island National Monument, Liberty Island, New York, NY 10004; 212-363-3200.

Circle Line Statue of Liberty Ferry, Inc., operates ferries to both monuments several times a day, departing from Battery Park in Manhattan and Liberty State Park in Jersey City, New Jersey. Round-trip fare: $6; $3 (under seventeen); $5 (seniors); 212-269-5755.

OFF-THE-BEATEN-PATH EXCURSIONS AND ATTRACTIONS

The Shorewalkers, a nonprofit organization dedicated to "exploring the city around its edges," has, since its 1982 founding, led walkers "along shores, through holes in fences, beneath reed forests, over rocks, and under bridges." Its weekly walks attract a crowd of old-timers and newcomers and tend to be informal and genial six-to-ten-mile waterside explorations. Recent excursions have included a walk over the Brooklyn Bridge led by flutists, an exploration of "wild and historic Jersey City," and a fifteen-mile hike along Staten Island's working waterfront. The annual "Great Saunter," a thirty-two-mile circumambulation of Manhattan, held in May, draws over 100 participants, about one quarter of whom usually complete the twelve- to fourteen-hour walk. Nonmembers are welcome on all hikes. A small contribution is requested from guests. Membership, which includes hike fees and a quarterly newsletter, is just $15 annually.

◆ **FOR MORE INFORMATION:** Shorewalkers, Box 20748, Cathedral Station, New York, NY 10025; 212-330-7686 for a recorded message of upcoming events.

Those who prefer less organized waterfront walking can do so at a number of parks and esplanades. Among them are the Brooklyn Heights Esplanade, Carl Schurz Park on Manhattan's upper East Side, Riverside Park on the Hudson north of 72nd Street, the pier walkways at South Street Seaport, Battery Park, and Battery Park City, where you can ogle (or charter for $2,000 for an afternoon) the luxury yachts docked in the ultra-fancy North Cove Yacht Harbor. According to a New York City/State plan now under development, a new Hudson River Park and esplanade will eventually extend from Battery Park City to 59th Street. An interim walkway/bikeway opened along part of this route in 1994. (For non-urban New York area walks, see Chapter 7).

FULTON FISH MARKET

Early risers with an interest in waterfront traditions should visit Manhattan's Fulton Fish Market after 3:00 a.m. on weekdays. Brusque conversations, hand signals, fancy knife-work, and fast action prevail as fishmongers sell thousands of pounds of salmon, snapper, tuna, and shellfish daily to buyers from the city's top restaurants and fish markets. Located adjacent to South Street

Explore the working waterfront in New York Harbor

Seaport at South and Fulton Streets, the market has operated at the same location since the early 1800s. Its East River docks once served a fleet of 300 fishing boats. Now, refrigerated trucks bring the fish in from other ports, but Fulton is still the largest and oldest wholesale fish market in the country. You can visit any morning before 8:00 a.m. on your own, but you will probably learn more if you join the South Street Seaport Museum's "Fish Before Work" tour from 6:00 to 7:30 a.m. on the first and third Thursdays of the month between April and October. Fee: $10; reservations required.

◆ **FOR MORE INFORMATION:** South Street Seaport Museum, 207 Front Street, New York, NY 10038; 212-788-8600.

GOVERNOR'S ISLAND

Governor's Island, the 170-acre island located just off the tip of Lower Manhattan, is Small Town USA with a Manhattan address. A U.S. Army property from 1794 until 1966 and now a U.S. Coast Guard base, the island has beautiful tree-lined streets with historic eighteenth- and nineteenth-century buildings, a public school, a movie theater, and a golf course. Historic forts that once defended the harbor now share the island with modern Coast Guard vessels that offer protection of a different sort. Sea buoys brought ashore for repairs line some of the waterside walkways, making the island an unusual and fascinating place to explore. Access is limited to the Coast Guard's annual open house, usually held during the summer, and a monthly walking tour of the island given by a private tour operator under contract with the Coast Guard. Otherwise, only those with official business are permitted on the ferry that leaves from the Battery.

◆ **FOR MORE INFORMATION:**

U.S. Coast Guard, Governor's Island, NY 10004; 212-668-3402.

Big Onion Walking Tours, Columbia University Post Office, P.O. Box 250201, New York, NY 10025; 212-794-0064.

BROOKLYN PIERS

In Red Hook, Brooklyn, two handsome Civil War–era warehouse piers have taken on new life as a lively neighborhood arts and business center. Developer Gregory O'Connell has brought an eclectic mix of small manufacturing businesses, museums, and arts facilities to the restored warehouses, Pier 41 and the Beard Street Pier. He expects to have a restaurant operating on site by summer 1995. Among the attractions are an annual summer arts festival sponsored by the Brooklyn Waterfront Arts Coalition, a trolley museum, and the Lehigh Valley Barge #79, a covered wooden railroad barge that is listed on the National Register of Historic Places as one of the last surviving examples of these once-numerous vessels. The barge serves as both a museum and a show-boat, which hosts many summer performances. Offering fabulous views of the Verrazano Narrows Bridge, the Statue of Liberty, and the Manhattan Skyline, the Red Hook piers are thus far two of the New York waterfront's best-kept secrets. Red Hook is accessible by subway and bus; a shuttle service operates for summer performances. Call for schedule and directions.

◆ **FOR MORE INFORMATION:** Pier 41/Beard Street Warehouse, 163 DeGraw Street, Brooklyn, NY 11231; 718-624-0160; Lehigh Valley Barge, 718-935-9019.

BARGEMUSIC

Bargemusic owner/impresario Olga Bloom saw the potential of converted barges two decades ago when a former coffee barge was put up for sale. "I thought it would be a perfect place for chamber music," she recalls. Bloom's floating concert hall, which is docked at Fulton Ferry Landing near the Brooklyn side of the Brooklyn Bridge, has been offering twice-weekly concerts since 1976. Tickets are $23; less for seniors and students. Refreshments are available.

◆ **FOR MORE INFORMATION:** Bargemusic, Fulton Ferry Landing, Brooklyn, NY 11201; 718-624-2083.

CHELSEA PIERS

Four turn-of-the-century ocean liner piers located on the Hudson River between 17th and 23rd Streets in Manhattan will reopen in 1995/96 as the Chelsea Piers Sports and Entertainment Complex, a multimillion-dollar facility that will house two indoor ice skating rinks, an outdoor in-line skating rink, a golf driving range, a gymnastics facility, a sports and fitness center, and film and television studios. The piers will also have a mile-long landscaped public esplanade, waterside restaurants, and an active boating and maritime center with tour boats, luxury charter boats, a sailing school, and a sea kayaking center. Several other vacant Hudson River piers are slated for future restoration as public open spaces as part of the city's and state's long-term plan for a new Hudson River park.

◆ **FOR MORE INFORMATION:**

Chelsea Piers Management, 936 Broadway, New York, NY 10010; 212-995-7660.

Hudson River Park Conservancy, 141 Fifth Avenue, New York, NY 10010; 212-353-0366.

SIGHTSEEING BOATS

Circle Line, which proclaims itself "America's Favorite Boat Ride," is certainly New York Harbor's best known and most comprehensive sightseeing cruise. Circling Manhattan Island, the three-hour, thirty-five-mile trip offers views of most of the city's notable landmarks and passes under nineteen bridges. Narrators provide lighthearted commentary on historical highlights and points of interest, with an emphasis on the residences of the rich and famous. The Circle Line is the only cruise that travels through the grittier sections of the upper Manhattan and Bronx waterways, passing by warehouses, blue-collar boat clubs, and beneath unusual-looking small bridges, including a historic aqueduct. To me, this backwater exploration is fascinating, but some passengers seem to regard it as a good opportunity for a nap. An onboard snack bar sells hot dogs, ice cream, snack food, cocktails, and souvenirs. Travelers' tip: Sit on the left side for the best view. A two-hour cruise that omits upper Manhattan operates on a limited schedule. Price: $18 (adults); $9 (children). Season: Daily sailings from late March until December.

◆ **FOR MORE INFORMATION:** Circle Line, Pier 83, 42nd Street and the Hudson River, New York, NY 10036; 212-563-3200.

Seaport Liberty Cruises, a Circle Line affiliate, operates one-hour sightseeing cruises, two-hour cocktail cruises, and weekend evening music cruises from Pier 16 at South Street Seaport. Price range: $12 to $20; children less.

◆ FOR MORE INFORMATION: Seaport Liberty Cruises, P.O. Box 864, New York, NY 10108; 212-630-8888.

Private ferries have made a comeback in New York Harbor and offer commuter trips between Manhattan and Brooklyn, Queens, and several New Jersey towns, with additional routes slated to begin in 1995 and 1996. During off-hours, two ferry companies operate ninety-minute New York Harbor sightseeing cruises, departing from Manhattan and Weehawken, New Jersey.

◆ FOR MORE INFORMATION:

Express Navigation, 2 First Avenue, Atlantic Highlands, NJ 07716; 800-BOATRIDE (800-262-8743).

New York Waterway, Pershing Road, Weehawken, NJ 07087; 800-533-3779.

New York City Department of Transportation, Office of Private Ferry Operations, Battery Maritime Building, New York, NY 10004; 212-806-6887.

The sailing vessels *Lettie G. Howard, Petrel, Pioneer,* and *Richard Robbins* offer passenger sails in New York Harbor, and several sailing schools and sailing clubs provide on-the-water opportunities (see Chapter 1).

DINING AFLOAT

World Yacht pioneered regularly scheduled dinner cruises in New York Harbor in 1984, and still offers the harbor's most sophisticated and upscale evening afloat. Each night, five nicely appointed picture-windowed vessels sail through the harbor, serving food, prepared by chefs hired away from some of the city's top restaurants, in an atmosphere enhanced by candlelight and live orchestra music. In addition to three-hour dinner cruises, which start at $62 per person, World Yacht, owned by Circle Line's parent company (New York Cruise Lines, Inc.) offers buffet lunch cruises starting at $27.50.

◆ **FOR MORE INFORMATION:** World Yacht Marina, Pier 81, West 41st Street and the Hudson River, New York, NY 10036; 212-630-8100.

Spirit Cruises, Inc. offers a meal, a stage show, live music, and dancing during its three-hour evening cruises. The emphasis is on spirited fun, rather than subdued sophistication, and guests seem to have a wonderful time. Two vessels — *Spirit of New York* and *Spirit of New Jersey* — offer lunch and dinner cruises from Manhattan and New Jersey, with prices starting under $30 for lunch and just over $50 for dinner.

◆ **FOR MORE INFORMATION:** Spirit Cruises, Inc., The Chelsea Piers, 23rd Street and the Hudson River, New York, NY 10011; 212-727-2789.

VIP Yacht Cruises' dinner, lunch and brunch cruises aboard the motor yachts *Royal Princess* and *Camelot* depart from North Cove Yacht Harbor at Battery Park City. International cuisine plus music and dancing are included in all cruises. Prices: $27.50 to $70 per person.

◆ **FOR MORE INFORMATION:** VIP Yacht Cruises, Inc., World Financial Center, 393 South End Avenue, New York, NY 10280; 718-934-1014.

Belle Ann Marie, an authentic 1925 Mississippi River stern-wheeler, offers once-a-month public dinner cruises on the Hudson River and New York Harbor from May until November. These four-hour cruises, complete with hors d'oeuvres, dinner, dessert, wine, beer, soft drinks, and Dixieland music ($55 per person), were instituted to give people the opportunity to ride on a vessel that is normally reserved for weddings and other private parties. The *Belle Ann Marie* sails out of Port Imperial Marina in Weehawken, New Jersey.

◆ **FOR MORE INFORMATION:** Dixieland Riverboat Company, P.O. Box 459, Madison, NJ 07940; 201-514-1829.

City Island

City Island, tucked into the far western corner of Long Island Sound, just two miles from the entrance to the East River, is one of New York's best surprises — a seafaring community with a New England atmosphere located fifteen miles east-northeast of mid-Manhattan, in the infamous Bronx.

This tiny island, less than a mile and a half long and just a half-mile wide at its broadest point, is really a world unto itself, with four yacht clubs, a half dozen marinas, two sailing schools, two sailmakers, twenty-five restaurants (most serving seafood), and, from its western shore, a fine view of the Manhattan skyline.

Although it has lost some of the glory it enjoyed when it was one of the premier boatbuilding centers in the United States (many America's Cup yachts were built here), City Island bustles with boating activity. It is home port to nearly 2,000 boats and a place where visitors can rent sailboats, take sailing lessons, or go out on a party boat for a day of fishing. The island hosts an active yacht racing program — about seventy sailboats participate in after-work races on Wednesday evenings from May through September — so it is an excellent place to watch or even find a boat to crew on.

The best way to see City Island is on foot; you could walk from one end to the other in about thirty minutes, but allow a few hours so you have time to visit the antique stores, galleries, and boutiques that have opened in recent years. For some real local color, be sure to stop at the North Wind Under Sea Institute and Trader John's.

Located in an 1875 sea captain's mansion at 610 City Island Avenue, the **North Wind Museum** offers a variety of hands-on exhibits to entertain and educate lovers of the sea. Among the displays are a life-size model of the head of a sperm whale, a fully equipped tugboat wheelhouse, and "The Undersea World of the Bronx," where visitors can view live specimens of local marine life, including lobsters, blue crabs, blackfish, starfish, killies, and porgies. A small admission fee is charged. Call 718-885-0701 for hours and information.

Trader John's, at 250 City Island Avenue, is a nautical junkyard and scavenger's paradise, so crammed with used cleats, blocks, and other treasures from the sea that you have to be an acrobat to get through the store. It is something you have to see to believe, but Trader John Persteins, who has been in business for more than thirty-five years, seems to know his stock and can point to some unusual marine antiques or useful replacement parts for your boat. There's no telephone ("He'd never be able to find it," a neighbor says) but the shop is easy to recognize — just look for the mooring balls on the sidewalk.

◆ **For sailing information:**

New York Sailing School, 231 Kirby Street, City Island, NY 10464; 718-885-3103. Boat rentals, sailing courses, evening cruises on a thirty-nine-foot sloop. Best buy: two-and-a-half-hour introductory sail for $25.

Lands End Sailing School, 560 Minneford Avenue, City Island, NY 10464; 718-885-2424. Lessons, rentals, captained Long Island Sound sailboat tours, and low-cost introductory sails.

Eastchester Bay Yacht Racing Association, City Island Yacht Club, 63 Pilot Street, City Island, NY 10464; 718-885-2487. Information on racing and crewing opportunities.

◆ **For fishing information:**

Apache Fishing Boat, 168 Fordham Street, City Island, NY; 718-885-0843. Daily fishing trips and moonlight charter cruises.

North Star, City Island Avenue, or, c/o Anderson, 15 Robins Road, Pleasantville, NY 10570; 718-822-0945. Daily fishing.

Riptide III, Jorgensen Landing, City Island, NY 10464; 718-885-0236. Daily fishing and evening charters.

Long Island's Gold Coast

Long Island's North Shore is Jay Gatsby's Gold Coast with mansions overlooking Long Island Sound and harbors filled with grand yachts. Before the Great Depression dimmed the region's opulence, many mansions contained a hundred rooms or more, and people snidely referred to the area between Manhasset and Huntington Bays as "the land of wretched excess." Gatsby's West Egg and East Egg, incidentally, are said to have been the towns of Great

Neck and Sands Point, which sit opposite one another on the shores of Manhasset Bay. Although the North Shore's largest mansions are gone, or gone to other uses, the coast is still dotted with elegant estates that can be admired from Long Island Sound.

The side-wheeler *Thomas Jefferson*, a modern diesel-powered replica of the steamboats that plied the sound during the nineteenth century, passes many of the mansions during its western Sound cruises, which depart from Glen Cove Marina off Hempstead Harbor. The *Jefferson,* which has classic lines and a staff dressed in period costumes, evokes old-time elegance on its regular brunch, dinner, and sightseeing cruises. Cruises start at $12 and top $100 for some events.

The 100-foot passenger yacht *Sterling,* which sails out of Port Washington, cruises by many mansions en route to New York Harbor during its nightly four-hour "Lady Liberty" dinner cruises. The boat leaves the sound and travels through the East River, past many Manhattan landmarks, to New York Harbor and the Statue of Liberty. The price ($59 to $79 per person) includes a buffet dinner, open bar, music, and dancing. A three-hour Sunday brunch cruise is $49.

◆ **FOR MORE INFORMATION:**
Thomas Jefferson, American Phoenix Lines, Inc., Glen Cove Marina, Glen Cove, NY 11542; 516-744-2353.

Sterling/Lady Liberty Cruises, 377 Jerusalem Avenue, Hempstead, NY 11550; 516-486-3057.

PORT WASHINGTON

The North Shore has many towns with a nautical flavor that are easily reached by car or by the Long Island Railroad. Port Washington on Manhasset Bay has several waterfront restaurants from which you can watch the always active harbor. The town's many yacht clubs sponsor sailboat races that often finish within view. It is especially pleasurable to sit inside a warm restaurant in mid-February and watch "frostbiters," as winter racers are called, compete in small sailing dinghies. The town dock is home to the "Pride of Cow Bay Nautical Museum," a rotating exhibit of nauti-

cal memorabilia displayed in a reconstructed tugboat pilothouse.
All viewing is through the portholes. Only "Port Hole Pete," the
Pop-Eye-like mannequin who stands at the wheel, is allowed inside.

◆ **FOR MORE INFORMATION:**

Port Washington Chamber of Commerce, P.O. Box 121,
Port Washington, NY 11050; 516-883-6566.

Long Island Convention and Visitors Bureau, Eisenhower
Park, 1899 Hempstead Turnpike, Suite 500, East Meadow, NY
11554; 516-794-4222

OYSTER BAY

Oyster Bay, a pretty yachting town with an oystering heritage, hosts Long Island's largest waterfront festival — the Oyster
Festival and Harborfest — which is held every October. The population of the tiny town swells to 200,000 as visitors come to enjoy
great food, entertainment, games, and contests. The festival also
pays tribute to the birthday of Oyster Bay's most illustrious former
resident, President Theodore Roosevelt. Sagamore Hill, Roosevelt's
beloved summer White House and his permanent residence from
1887 until his death in 1919, is located on Oyster Bay's Cove
Neck. This twenty-three-room Victorian home is now a museum,
run by the National Park Service, which recalls Roosevelt's personality and achievements. House tours are given hourly from 9:00
a.m. to 4:00 p.m. Open year-round. Tickets: $2; children under 16
free

◆ **FOR MORE INFORMATION:**

Oyster Bay Chamber of Commerce, 120 South Street,
Oyster Bay, NY 11771; 516-624-8082.

Sagamore Hill, Cove Neck Road, Oyster Bay, NY 11771;
516-922-4447.

COLD SPRING HARBOR

In the mid-nineteenth century, Cold Spring Harbor, with
its 500 residents and nine-ship whaling fleet, was Long Island's second largest whaling port. Today the town is a colonial-style village
with boutiques, galleries, whaling-era buildings, and a harbor filled

with yachts. The Cold Spring Harbor Whaling Museum (see Chapter 2) keeps traditions alive with exhibits and special programs, including a monthly walking tour of "Bedlam Street," as Main Street was called in the days when whalemen celebrated there, no holds barred, on their return from years at sea. The Cold Spring Harbor Fish Hatchery and Aquarium (see Chapter 7) is also a local attraction worth visiting.

♦ FOR MORE INFORMATION:

Cold Spring Harbor Whaling Museum, 516-367-3418.

Cold Spring Harbor Fish Hatchery and Aquarium, 516-692-6768.

VANDERBILT MUSEUM AND PLANETARIUM

From the porch of Eagle's Nest, William K. Vanderbilt II's twenty-four-room Spanish Revival–style mansion, one can imagine what Long Island's Gilded Age must have been like. Situated on a bluff overlooking Long Island Sound and Northport Harbor (where Vanderbilt kept his yacht, *Alva*), the mansion has stunning views and a beautiful interior with carved marble fireplaces, elaborate ceilings and staircases, lavish furniture, and wonderful art. The great-grandson of tycoon and yachtsman Commodore Cornelius Vanderbilt, William K. Vanderbilt II (1878–1944) left his forty-three-acre estate and an endowment for its upkeep to Suffolk County for use as a museum. The museum houses 17,000 marine science and natural history specimens and one of the largest planetariums in the United States, which features regular sky shows and weekend laser and pop music presentations. Open Tuesday through Saturday, year-round. Small admission fee.

♦ FOR MORE INFORMATION: Suffolk County Vanderbilt Museum and Planetarium, 180 Little Neck Road, Centerport, NY 11721; 516-854-5555.

EATON'S NECK LIGHTHOUSE

Eaton's Neck Lighthouse, a handsome sandstone octagon pyramid that overlooks Long Island Sound from the northernmost spit of land in the town of Northport, is Long Island's second oldest

lighthouse (Montauk Light is two years older). Now part of an
active U.S. Coast Guard Station, Eaton's Neck Light has been in
continuous service since its whale-oil lanterns were first lit in 1799.
The tower, which is 73 feet above ground and 144 feet above the
water, alerts mariners to what are said to be Long Island Sound's
most treacherous reefs. The now-automated light is listed on the
National Register of Historic Places, and is open to visitors by
appointment. Those wishing to tour the lighthouse should submit a
written request to the commanding officer of the Eaton's Neck
Coast Guard station at least two weeks in advance.

◆ **FOR MORE INFORMATION:** U.S. Coast Guard,
Eaton's Neck Station, Lighthouse Road, Northport, NY 11768;
516-261-6959.

P. T. BARNUM'S BOAT

The Bridgeport and Port Jefferson Steamboat Company
has show business in its genes. One of its original stockholders was
nineteenth-century showman P. T. Barnum, who, with homes in
both Bridgeport and Port Jefferson, wanted an easy way to travel,
and persuaded friends to start the ferry service in 1883. Today, the
company's ferries — *Park City* and *Grand Republic* — carry up to
100 cars and 1,000 passengers fourteen miles across Long Island
Sound in ninety minutes, year-round, saving 105 miles of driving.
Weekends are show time, when the ferries run moonlight cruises
and passengers dance to the music of a 1950s band. Moonlight
cruises leave from Port Jefferson and cost $15. Reservations
required. Regular ferry rates (subject to change) are $11 for foot
passengers and start at $26 for autos. Note: Ferry travelers can tour
the Barnum Museum in Bridgeport and the Barnum home in Port
Jefferson.

◆ **FOR MORE INFORMATION:** Bridgeport and Port
Jefferson Steamboat Co., 102 West Broadway, Port Jefferson, NY
17777; 516-473-0286.

The North Fork

"Discover the tranquillity of the North Fork, a place suspended in time," a Long Island travel ad says, showing a picture of

three baymen standing knee deep in calm water, clam rakes in their hands, their catch in baskets floating beside them. "Our heritage is our present day reality."

The ad, of course, is an overstatement. The North Fork has changed a great deal since the days of whaling ships, busy shipyards, and shellfish so plentiful they could support whole communities. But the area retains a wholesome simplicity with strong connections to the sea that makes it fascinating to explore. A deepwater commercial fishing fleet operates out of Greenport, baymen

Long Island's Fishtail

During the last Ice Age, about 15,000 years ago, massive glaciers advanced along the East Coast, shifting sand and rocks and shoving the land at Long Island's eastern end into two distinct forks. Seen from above, the configuration resembles the tail of a giant fish. Hence, "Fishtail," a favorite nickname for the East End. (The fish's mouth, incidentally, is Jamaica Bay in New York Harbor.)

These forks, which are separated from one another by bays and islands, differ in character, both geologically and socially. The North Fork, part of what geologists call the Harbor Hill Moraine, extends eastward twenty-eight miles from Riverhead to Orient Point. High bluffs and pebbly, boulder-strewn beaches characterize its Long Island Sound shore, and its towns retain a rural farm and fishing village atmosphere. Permanent residents outnumber vacationers here.

The South Fork, forty-four miles long, includes the Hamptons and Montauk and is part of a different geologic formation known as the Ronkonkoma Moraine. Its miles of sandy, dune-backed ocean beaches have made the area one of the trendiest and wealthiest summer communities on the East Coast.

still fish for scallops and clams, new passenger vessels are giving sightseeing tours, pleasure boats fill the harbors, and new maritime museums and restored lighthouses keep traditions alive.

RIVERHEAD

In Riverhead, the *Peconic River Lady*, an eighty-five-foot paddle-wheel dinner boat, is the first of several planned attractions that are bringing new life to the riverfront. Okeanos Foundation, a widely respected marine research and education center, was set to break ground on the banks of the Peconic River before the end of 1994 for an 80,000-square-foot aquarium. The aquarium, which is scheduled for a 1997 opening, will house major sea life exhibits, as well as a marine mammal rehabilitation and release area that will be open to the public. Another not-for-profit group is trying to raise funds for the construction of a major maritime museum in Riverhead.

In the meantime, visitors can enjoy wildlife areas, rural scenery, and beautiful homes as they cruise aboard the *Peconic River Lady* from Riverhead to Peconic Bay. Lunch and dinner cruises feature buffet dining and live entertainment. Prices: $30 to $50. Reservations required.

For those who prefer exploring on their own, the **Peconic Paddler** has been renting canoes and sea kayaks out of a converted gas station next to the river in Riverhead for nearly two decades. Its owner, Jim Dreeban, an expert on local waters, arranges guided tours and provides land transportation to the best river canoeing spots. He also recommends top sea kayaking areas in Peconic Bay.

◆ FOR MORE INFORMATION:

Peconic River Lady, Riverhead Village Pier, Riverhead, NY 11901; 516-369-3700.

The Peconic Paddler, 89 Peconic Avenue, Riverhead, NY 11901; 516-727-9585.

HORTON POINT LIGHTHOUSE

The Horton Point Lighthouse, overlooking Long Island Sound in the town of Southold, is a North Fork treasure. The light, which warns mariners away from rocky Dead Man's Cove, traces its lineage to George Washington, who, as a young surveyor in 1757, recommended a navigational light at that location. It was another hundred years, however, before the light's whale-oil lamp glowed for the first time.

The structure itself, a modest 49-foot tower attached to a keeper's house, sits atop a 110-foot bluff offering a wonderful panorama of Long Island Sound. A museum in the keeper's house displays lighthouse logs going back to 1857, as well as a splendid collection of nineteenth-century whaling artifacts, with ships' logs, sailors' journals, sea chests, tools, scrimshaw, and other articles portraying the life of Southold's mariners. All of this has been put together by local residents who donated or lent heirlooms to the museum and spearheaded the effort to restore the lighthouse, which had been vandalized after decommissioning by the Coast Guard in 1933. In tribute to the success of the restoration effort, the Coast Guard reactivated Horton Point Lighthouse in 1990.

Horton Point itself is a grand spot. A grassy park with flowering trees surrounds the lighthouse and is the site of a summer concert series. Mammoth boulders dating from the Ice Age lie on the beach below, which you can explore by descending a staircase from the top of the bluff.

The lighthouse and museum are open for visitors summer weekends from 11:30 a.m. to 4:00 p.m. Donation requested.

◆ **FOR MORE INFORMATION:** Horton Point Lighthouse and Nautical Museum, Lighthouse Road, P.O. Box 1, Southold, NY 11971; 516-765-5500.

GREENPORT

Greenport, the North Fork's maritime hub, has the feel of a New England fishing village. Walk along the waterfront and you will see large commercial fishing boats unloading their catch, the 1906 fishing schooner *Mary E.* heading out for a day sail with a load of passengers (see Chapter 1), the historic three-masted barkentine *Regina Maris* (see Chapter 2) welcoming visitors and volunteers, and cruisers arriving by boat to dine at Claudio's, a seafood restaurant operated by the same family since 1870 (516-477-0627).

An active seaport and shipbuilding center since the seventeenth century, Greenport was a prime fishing and trading center, a port of call for whaling ships, a transfer point for travelers heading to New England by boat, and, during Prohibition, a hot rum-running spot. Its shipyards built minesweepers during World War II, and its sailors assisted the U.S. Navy by patrolling the coast in their wooden sailboats (see Chapter 2).

Beautiful homes and unusual shops make Greenport fun to explore on foot. Be sure to find your way to the East End Seaport Maritime Museum (see Chapter 2), located in the old railroad station, and to Preston's, the oldest ship's chandlery in the United States. Founded by a retired sea captain in 1880, Preston's, located

Bug Lighthouse is familiar to anyone sailing through Gardiners Bay from Long Island Sound or the Atlantic

on Main Street Wharf (516-477-1990), sells everything from marine hardware and foul weather gear to books and nautical prints. You are also likely to find some old ships' figureheads, cannons, and treasure chests displayed in the store.

From nearby docks, *Rebecca Lee,* billed as the only "real" stern-wheeler cruising out of Long Island, offers ninety-minute sightseeing cruises and two-hour wine-and-cheese sunset cruises. Price: $10 (sightseeing); $20 (sunset). The *Peconic Star II,* a ninety-passenger party boat, takes daily fishing trips and offers occasional moonlight cruises. The Greenport Chamber of Commerce has information about charter fishing excursions.

◆ **FOR MORE INFORMATION:**

Rebecca Lee, 2805 West Mill Road, Mattituck, NY 11952; 516-298-3278.

Peconic Star II, D. B. Fishing Corporation, 254 Falcon Avenue, Patchogue, NY 11772; 516-289-6899.

Greenport Chamber of Commerce, P.O. Box 66, Greenport, NY 11944; 516-477-1383.

ORIENT POINT

Orient Point, at the North Fork's far east end, is worth a visit if only to walk along the beach to the spit of land that overlooks Plum Gut, where the waters of Long Island Sound and Gardiners Bay meet in a great tidal rip. Anyone who has ever piloted a boat through the gut's tricky waters will enjoy looking at its "coffee pot" lighthouse from the security of shore and watching the thousands of seabirds that converge on Plum Island, a U.S. Department of Agriculture Animal Study Center.

Orient also has a small, sleepy village, a wonderful beach on Gardiners Bay — at the 342-acre Orient Beach State Park — party fishing boats, and the terminal of the Cross Sound Ferry.

The **Cross Sound Ferry** has four large car-carrying and passenger vessels that make the approximately ninety-minute trip between Orient Point and New London, Connecticut, several times a day, year-round. Prices: passengers (one way), $8.50; autos, $28. The open fishing boat *Prime Time III* sails daily from Orient by the

Sea Marina, one block west of the ferry terminal, and several charter fishing boats operate from the area.

◆ **FOR MORE INFORMATION:**

Cross Sound Ferry, 2 Ferry Street, P.O. Box 33, New London, CT 06320; 203-443-5281 or 516-323-2525.

Prime Time III, Orient by the Sea Marina, Orient Point,
NY 11952; 516-323-2618.

WINERY TOURS

The North Fork's connections to the sea remain strong, but
in recent years potato farms-turned-vineyards have given the area a
new identity as a wine region that is beginning to rival California's
Sonoma and Napa Valleys. Since the 1970s, when Alex and Louisa
Hargrave planted the area's first vines, hundreds of acres of vineyards have been established, and more than a dozen wineries have
opened, boosting the local economy and bringing visitors for tours
and tastings. Many of the wineries, which are located on Main
Road (Route 25), hang out welcome signs, and local tourist offices
have winery guides.

◆ **FOR MORE INFORMATION:** Long Island Wine
Council, 1281 Old Country Road, Riverhead, NY 11901; 516-
475-5492.

Shelter Island

Nestled between the flukes of Long Island's Fishtail, less
than a mile from Greenport and just a half mile from the town of
North Haven on the South Fork, Shelter Island is a world apart. Its
earliest inhabitants, the Manhanset Indians, called it "manhansack-
ahaquash awamock" — island sheltered by islands. And to this day,
it remains a quiet place, sheltered from the hubbub of nearby East
End resorts by a buffer zone of bays.

But rest assured, visitors are welcome. Car ferries from
Greenport and North Haven operate on a regular schedule
throughout the year, carrying people to first-class restaurants and
inns, uncrowded beaches, beautiful harbors, and a nature preserve

that encompasses more than one quarter of the land on Shelter Island.

The 8,000-square-acre island is a Rorschach blot of coves and twisting coastline, roughly six miles long by four miles wide, that calls out for exploration. You can drive along its uncrowded roads (maximum speed 35 mph), but bicycles are the vehicle of choice. Piccozzi's (516-749-0045) in Shelter Island Heights has been renting them since 1927.

Wherever you go on this island you are likely to find something that pleases: eclectic architecture that ranges from New England classic to Queen Anne Victorian, handsome yachts, classic small boats, large stands of oak, and long stretches of empty beach. Seek out Dering Harbor, a hub of water activity, and Shelter Island Heights, the 1871 home of the Shelter Island Grove and Camp Meeting Association of the Methodist Episcopal Church. Its members' "cottages," decorated with ornate gingerbread trim, are some of the island's most unusual buildings.

Shelter Island's most remarkable site, however, is the **Mashomack Preserve**, 2,100 acres of woodlands and wetlands, owned and maintained in a forever-wild state by the Nature Conservancy, which purchased the land in 1980 to stop development and to protect its unusually large osprey population. Four trails, ranging from one and a half to eleven miles, are open to hikers from 9:00 a.m. to 5:00 p.m. every day except Tuesdays.

◆ FOR MORE INFORMATION: Mashomack Preserve, P.O. Box 850, Shelter Island, NY 11964; 516-749-1001.

Shelter Island's ferries, which have been operating from the same locations for more than two centuries, run year-round from 6:00 a.m. until 11:45 p.m. (longer hours in summer). Prices: North Ferry: $6.50 one-way, car and driver, $7 same-day round-trip, $1 each additional passenger. South Ferry: $6 one way, $6.50 round-trip, $1 each additional passenger.

◆ FOR MORE INFORMATION:
Shelter Island Chamber of Commerce, Box 598, Shelter Island, NY 11964; 516-749-0399.

North Ferry (Greenport to Shelter Island), Shelter Island Heights, NY 11965; 516-749-0139.

South Ferry (North Haven to Shelter Island), Box 614, Shelter Island, NY 11964; 516-740-0007.

The South Fork and Montauk

SAG HARBOR

Sag Harbor, an old whaling village with twisting streets lined with pretty shingled houses and stately captains' homes, is a good place to begin a visit to Long Island's South Fork. Known as the "un-Hamptons Hampton," the town offers an opportunity to see the East End's southern peninsula from a different perspective. Best known for its wide, sandy Atlantic Ocean beaches and trendy Hampton communities, the South Fork also has historic port towns, farmlands, protected wildlife areas, salt marshes, beautiful bays, and, at Montauk, New York's most famous lighthouse.

Overlooking Shelter Island and Gardiners Bay, Sag Harbor was a prominent eighteenth-century shipbuilding center and seaport. Declared an official U.S. Port of Entry by George Washington in 1789, Sag Harbor at one time handled more shipping tonnage than New York Harbor, and in the nineteenth century, it was the country's third busiest whaling port. The Sag Harbor Whaling and Historical Museum (see Chapter 2) commemorates the history of this era when more than 500 whaling voyages sailed from or returned to the town.

Sag Harbor's prominence as a whaling center ended abruptly in the 1850s, however. When the 1849 California Gold Rush offered a seemingly easier way to find a fortune, many whalers sailed for San Francisco and never came back. Finally, the 1855 discovery of crude oil in Pennsylvania ended the demand for whale oil. But the town continued as an important fishing port for some time.

Now a National Historic District, Sag Harbor retains a salty flavor and a comfortable small-town atmosphere. Nineteenth-century buildings along Main Street currently house restaurants, antique shops, bookstores, and boutiques, many selling nautical items. Sag Harbor's historic docks have been rebuilt as a modern marina with a dockside restaurant with indoor and outdoor seating.

American Beauty, a forty-five-foot sightseeing boat, sails from Long Wharf, offering ninety-minute tours of Peconic and Gardiners Bays. Captain Don Heckman, a former commercial fisherman with a passion for the marine environment, gives a narration that highlights the history and ecological importance of the area. Three-hour sunset cruises circumnavigate Shelter Island. Prices: $15 and up; discounts for kids, family groups.

◆ **FOR MORE INFORMATION:**

Sag Harbor Chamber of Commerce, P.O. Box 2810, Sag Harbor, NY 11963; 516-725-0011.

American Beauty, Harbor Tours, Inc., P.O. Box 7, Sag Harbor, NY 11963; 516-728-7310.

PRISTINE BAYS

The Peconic/Gardiners Bay area, designated for inclusion in the National Estuary Program, has a pristine natural beauty that is worth exploring either by boat or along the shore by car, bicycle, or on foot. Here you will find uncrowded coves where baymen have worked for centuries and still go out in scallop boats or fishing dories that you may see pulled up on the shore. Tiny Acabonack Harbor in Springs, near East Hampton, is particularly unspoiled and worth seeking out.

From there, you'll also have a good view of Gardiners Island, a large, mostly uninhabited private island that Lion Gardiner bought from the Montauket Indians in 1639. A royal grant later stipulated that it should remain in the same family forever, and so far, it has. The 3,300-acre island has meadows and woodlands that serve as a sanctuary for birds and other wildlife, including one of the largest osprey populations in the Northeast. Boaters can see a windmill dating from 1815 on the island's west side. There is also a mansion, a small airport, and reportedly a caretaker with a gun who is quite effective in keeping uninvited guests away. While you can't visit his island, should you be interested, you can visit Lion Gardiner's grave in the cemetery in the center of the town of East Hampton.

OCEAN BEACHES

The South Fork's ocean beaches are the region's biggest draw, and deservedly so. They are wonderful. Part of a littoral chain that extends from the Rockaways in New York City to Montauk Point, these East End beaches are among the best in the nation. The only problem is access. Most beaches either require resident stickers, nonresident parking stickers ($100 and up for the season), or limited one-day parking permits ($10 and up). Call local chambers of commerce for information, or head straight for Hither Hills State Park in Montauk, which has a broad, clean, two-mile-long ocean beach (parking $4), plus a camping area with nature trails, guided walks, and special programs.

◆ FOR MORE INFORMATION:

East Hampton Chamber of Commerce, Park Place, East Hampton, NY 11937; 516-324-0362.

Southampton Chamber of Commerce, 76 Main Street, Southampton, NY 11968; 516-283-0402.

Hither Hills State Park, Montauk Highway, Montauk, NY 11954; 516-668-2554.

MONTAUK LIGHTHOUSE

Montauk Point, an ocean-gouged bluff at the easternmost point in New York State, is an awesome manifestation of the unrelenting power of the sea. When the lighthouse that stands on top of it was lit for the first time in 1797, it was 297 feet back from the shore; today Montauk Lighthouse is only 50 feet from the edge. Preservationists are battling time and tide with a promising but expensive erosion control program, but the outcome of this man vs. nature race is too close to call. In the future, the lighthouse may have to be moved to prevent it from toppling into the sea.

In the meantime, New York state's oldest lighthouse offers both unparalleled coastal and ocean views and fascinating historical insights. The 108-foot tower, painted white with a broad brown band, has been doing its job for nearly two centuries, although there have been some minor changes along the way. Now containing an automated light operated as an aid to navigation by the U.S. Coast Guard, Montauk Lighthouse is maintained by the Montauk Historical Society, which invites visitors to climb the 137-step spiral staircase to the top and to view an excellent display of lighthouse artifacts in an on-site museum. Highlights include drawings and paintings dating back to 1797, logs from the 1830s, and the Fresnel lens, made of concentric glass prisms, that provided the light's beacon from 1904 until 1987. A copy of President George Washington's authorization to construct the light, dated April 12, 1792, hangs in the museum, and a video narrated by Dick Cavett provides interesting details.

An exhibit on the effort to "Hold Up the Bank" with a terracing system of erosion control is particularly compelling, as is the cost — $1,000 per foot — but the effort has earned wide support. An annual Paul Simon charity concert, held at a nearby ranch, has raised hundreds of thousands of dollars for the effort. The lighthouse is open daily during the summer, and weekends only from November through March. Small admission charge.

◆ **FOR MORE INFORMATION:** Montauk Point Lighthouse, RFD 2, Box 112, Montauk, NY 11954; 516-668-2544.

MONTAUK ACTIVITIES

Montauk itself is a ten-mile-long, two-mile-wide peninsula with thirty miles of ocean and bay beaches, and three state parks — Hither Hills, Montauk Point, and Montauk Downs — which, in addition to beaches, offer nature trails, camping, tennis, and golf. In Montauk, you can rent a horse from the oldest cattle ranch in the United States and go riding on the beach, or you can take a fishing trip from the harbor that claims to be the "Sportfishing Capital of the World."

Dozens of charter and party boats share the harbor area at Lake Montauk, about four miles back from the point, with a large commercial fishing fleet. Fishing boats offer trips lasting from nearshore half-days to three-day offshore expeditions. The harbor also has a number of seafood restaurants and is the departure point for ferries to Block Island, Rhode Island, and New London, Connecticut, as well as whale watching cruises, run by the Okeanos Ocean Research Foundation (see Chapter 7).

◆ **FOR MORE INFORMATION:**

Montauk Chamber of Commerce, P.O. 5029, Montauk, NY 11954; 516-668-2428.

New York State Parks, Long Island Region, P.O. Box 247, Babylon, NY 11702; 516-669-1000.

Deep Hollow Ranch, P.O. Box 835, Montauk, NY 11954; 516-668-2744.

The Viking Fleet (ferries and fishing trips), RD1, P.O. Box 259, West Lake Drive, Montauk, NY 11954; 516-668-5709 or 800-MONTAUK.

Lazy Bones (open fishing boat), Johnny Marlin's Dock, Montauk, NY 11954; 516-688-5671.

Marlin V, Montauk Harbor, Montauk, NY 11954; 516-668-5343 or 718-845-8082.

Fire Island

Fire Island, a thirty-two-mile-long strip of sand and dunes three miles off Long Island's South Shore, is a place of many identities. Designated a National Seashore in 1964, this fragile and ever-changing barrier island has large beachfront parks at either end, a seven-mile-long protected wilderness, nature trails under the care of the National Park Service, a historic lighthouse, and seventeen summer colonies — each with a personality so distinct that you need a scorecard to keep track.

Fortunately, the *Fire Island Times* publishes one every week. A fanciful map on the tabloid's inside back cover is accompanied by thumbnail descriptions that steer you to a community that suits your taste. It tells you that: Fair Harbor attracts upscale advertising and publishing types; Fire Island Pines, the most beautiful community, has "roller coaster sidewalks"; Ocean Beach has more houses, people, hotels, bars, and restaurants than anyplace else; predominately gay Cherry Grove is noted for its theater, art shows, shops, restaurants, and whimsical house styles; and Point O' Woods, the most exclusive community, fences out its neighbors and frowns on uninvited guests.

Some places are quiet and family oriented, others are artsy and flamboyant, and still others are party towns where group renters concentrate on volleyball and beer. What links these diverse communities is an unbroken expanse of one of the best beaches on the East Coast and a common devotion to an island lifestyle.

Although it is possible to drive to beach parking areas at the island's east and west extremes, Fire Island proper is car free. Ferries serving different Fire Island docks depart from three South Shore towns — Bay Shore, Sayville, and Patchogue — the twenty-five-minute Great South Bay crossing giving passengers a chance to shed their mainland tensions. On the island, people travel by foot along wooden walkways or sandy paths, using small red wagons to carry their groceries and gear. The distances are generally not far, since at Fire Island's widest point, it is just a half mile from the ocean to the bay. Water taxis provide transportation between communities.

Fire Island's private colonies are small and generally occupied by homeowners or seasonal renters, so tourist facilities are scarce. But don't let that put you off. It is possible to hop on a ferry, enjoy the beach, explore by water taxi, or just walk around and experience some of the island's colorful ambiance and culture. Ocean Beach and Ocean Bay Park are good starting points since both have bars, restaurants, and hotels that welcome guests.

◆ **FOR MORE INFORMATION:** Fire Island Tourism Office; 516-563-8448.

According to the National Park Service, which oversees the Fire Island National Seashore, about five million people visit every year. Most of these bypass the private communities and head directly to the beaches and wildlife areas that make up nearly 80 percent of the island. From west to east, these include the following.

ROBERT MOSES STATE PARK

Robert Moses State Park, a 1,000-acre area with a broad, flat beach, is accessible by car from the town of Babylon via the Robert Moses Causeway. It has public parking, as well as bathhouses, a picnic ground, and refreshment stands. You can park here and walk about a half mile to the Fire Island Lighthouse. Open year-round. Parking fee from Memorial Day to Labor Day.

FIRE ISLAND LIGHTHOUSE

When the Fire Island Lighthouse was first lit in 1858, it stood at the island's western tip. Now, as a result of the constant westward shift of sand, the black-and-white light tower is five miles back from the point. Threatened with demolition after it was taken out of Coast Guard Service in 1974, this lighthouse (like many others in New York and New Jersey) was saved by citizens who, in this case, raised over $1 million for its restoration. Its powerful light began flashing again in 1986, and the 192-step tower and a small museum in the adjacent keeper's quarters are open for visitors on various schedules from spring through fall.

The National Park Service, which has a station on site, gives historical presentations, leads nature walks, and runs fishing and craft programs for children. The still active Fire Island Lighthouse Preservation Society maintains the structure and sponsors special events, the most notable being the Barefoot and Black Tie Gala, a fundraiser and party held at the lighthouse every August. Access: From the easternmost parking lot at Robert Moses State Park, walk east about half a mile; or take the ferry from Bay Shore, Long Island, to the town of Kismet and walk one mile west. Special auto access is available for handicapped visitors. Admission free, donations welcomed.

SAILORS HAVEN/SUNKEN FOREST

Sailors Haven/Sunken Forest, a National Seashore area accessible by ferry from Sayville, has both a superb ocean beach and a remarkable maritime hardwood forest hidden behind forty-foot dunes. Trails covered by wooden walkways wind for a mile and a half beneath a dense canopy of holly, tupelo and sassafras trees that grow to the height of the dunes, while ferns and vines (including poison ivy) cover the forest floor. This is a wonderfully cool and shaded wildlife area where deer and rabbits live in abundance. The Park Service operates a visitors center with "please-touch" exhibits, bathhouses, and refreshments. The ferry dock and small boat marina are nearby.

WATCH HILL

If you are lucky enough to win a lottery, you can camp at one of the twenty-six campsites operated by the National Park Service at Watch Hill, an area just to the east of the last residential community. Stays are limited to four nights, and if there are more applications than tent sites (which is often the case), campers are selected by lot. In addition to the camping facilities, Watch Hill has a beach and visitors center open to day-trippers.

FIRE ISLAND NATIONAL WILDERNESS AREA

The Fire Island National Wilderness Area begins at Watch Hill and extends eastward seven miles to Smith Point West. Congress designated this incredible stretch of beach, dunes, and bay areas as a protected wilderness in 1980. The only area in New York State to be so honored, it is open to hikers who want to explore a primitive landscape that looks as it did centuries ago. Access is from Patchogue, via ferry to Watch Hill or by car via a bridge to Smith Point. Smith Point has another National Park Service visitors center with exhibits, a nature trail, park ranger programs, and guided walks. The Smith Point County Park is at the east and extends to the end of the island at Moriches inlet.

◆ **FOR MORE INFORMATION:**
Robert Moses State Park, 516-669-0449.

Fire Island Lighthouse Preservation Society, Inc., Captree Island, Box C-8, Babylon, NY 11702; 516-312-7033.

Fire Island National Seashore, 120 Laurel Street, Patchogue, NY 11772; 516-661-4876.

Sailors Haven Visitors Center, 516-597-6183.

Watch Hill Access, 516-597-6455.

Smith Point West Access, 516-281-3010.

FERRY SERVICE

Regular ferry service to Fire Island dates back to the late nineteenth century when the first summer colonies and large hotels began operation. The first ferries were sailboats that operated on a fairly casual schedule; after that came converted yachts, then former rum-running boats and surplus navy craft. Today's fleet includes modern ferries built specifically for the Great South Bay transit, as well as a few of the old classics.

◆ FOR MORE INFORMATION:

Fire Island Ferries, Inc., operates from Bay Shore to the following Fire Island communities: Kismet, Saltaire, Fair Harbor, Dunewood, Ocean Beach, Seaview, and Ocean Bay Park. Boats operate on frequent (usually hourly schedules) from Memorial Day through Labor Day, and continue limited service to Ocean Beach through the winter, ice conditions permitting. Round-trip fare: $10.50 adults, $5 children. Additional daily parking fee at ferry terminal. P.O. Box P311, Bay Shore, NY, 11706; 516-665-3600.

Sayville Ferry Service, Inc., runs from Sayville to Fire Island Pines, Cherry Grove, and Sailors Haven/Sunken Forest. Frequent daily service from March through December; limited weekend service the remainder of the year, conditions permitting. Round-trip fare: $10 adults, $5 children. Sunken Forest route (May to October only): $8 adults, $4.50 children. Parking extra. P.O. Box 626, Sayville, NY 11782; 516-589-0810.

Davis Park Ferry Company runs from Patchogue to Davis Park and Watch Hill, mid-March through November. One-way fare: $5.50 adults, $3.25 children. Parking extra. P.O. Box 998, Patchogue, NY 17772; 516-475-1665.

GREAT SOUTH BAY

Great South Bay, the shallow body of water between Fire Island and mainland Long Island, once a prosperous oystering area (see Long Island Maritime Museum, Chapter 2), remains an active center for fishing and recreational boating. Sightseeing/dinner cruise boats and open fishing boats operate in the area.

The *Evening Star*, operated by Fire Island Ferries, is a three-deck dinner boat that offers lunch, brunch, and special themed party cruises — murder mystery nights, Fifties nights, and so on — through Great South Bay. A once-a-week excursion to Fire Island Lighthouse is a popular summer option. Prices: $25 to $40. The *Bay Mist*, a 200-passenger dinner boat, runs lunch and dinner dance cruises from Patchogue. Prices start at $25. Captree State Park Ferries runs one-and-a-half-hour sightseeing cruises of Great South Bay during the summer and weekly evening music cruises. Several charter and open fishing boats also leave from Captree State Park.

◆ **FOR MORE INFORMATION:**

Evening Star, P.O. Box P311, Bay Shore, NY 11707; 515-666-3601.

Bay Mist, Great South Bay Excursion, Inc., P.O. Box 814, Patchogue, NY 11772; 516-475-1606 or 800-310-7234.

Captree State Park Ferries, Babylon, NY 11707; 516-661-5061.

Captree Boatman's Association, Captree State Park, Box 5372, Babylon, NY 11707; 516-669-6464.

New Jersey

Sandy Hook and Environs

The fixed white beam of Sandy Hook Lighthouse, the oldest continuously operating lighthouse in the United States, has been guiding mariners into the Port of New York since 1764. Built at the request of New York merchants, who were tired of being victims of the New Jersey shoals that claimed too many of their ships, the 103-foot-tall lighthouse was an immediate aid to sailors approaching the coast. Today, its 60,000-candlepower light can be seen nineteen miles offshore. The lighthouse's interior is not open to visitors, but it is impressive, nonetheless, just to stand and look at a structure that has been doing the same job since before this country was a nation.

The lighthouse is only one of several good reasons to visit Sandy Hook, a six-and-a-half-mile-long sand peninsula at the northern end of New Jersey's ocean coast. Part of the Gateway National Recreation Area, which was established in 1972, Sandy Hook contains miles of dunes and ocean beaches (including one that welcomes nude sunbathers), rich wildlife habitats, a small museum, an old army fort, and, legend has it, treasure buried by Captain Kidd. It is a splendid natural oasis in the center of a dense urban area, a point that is dramatically underscored when you walk barefoot on north beach and look out at the Manhattan skyline in the distance.

On weekend beach days, the parking lots are often filled by 10:00 a.m., and car entry is barred thereafter. So, go early, or better yet, go another time. Sandy Hook is open year-round, and spring and fall are the best seasons to walk along the dune trails and watch migrating birds. Alternatively, you could try "Going Bunkers" and tour Sandy Hook's forts and gun batteries. Park rangers, who lead a variety of special programs throughout the year, recommend flashlights and sturdy shoes for this two-hour bunker tour. Other programs include canoe trips, tours of Sandy Hook's remarkable holly forest, ship-rescue demonstrations, craft and music festivals, and marsh walks (bring mosquito repellent).

Sandy Hook owes its substantial areas of open, undeveloped shorefront to the U.S. Army, which maintained coastal defense forts there from the Revolutionary War until 1974 and then turned the property over to the National Park Service when it was no longer needed. Besides the lighthouse and gun batteries, Fort Hancock (1895–1974), near the peninsula's northern end, includes handsome Georgian Revival captains' homes, more modest soldiers' housing, an old jail now occupied by the Sandy Hook Museum, and a former Nike missile site.

You can pick up a brochure for a self-guided tour of this and other areas at the National Park Service visitors center located in an 1894 U.S. Lifesaving Station at Spermaceti Cove, about two miles in from the park entrance.

◆ **FOR MORE INFORMATION:** Gateway National Recreation Area, Sandy Hook Unit, P.O. Box 530, Fort Hancock, NJ 07732; 908-872-0115.

TWIN LIGHTS

For a spectacular view of New Jersey's north coast, head for the Twin Lights of the Navesink, located on a bluff overlooking the ocean and the Shrewsbury River in Highlands. At 200 feet above sea level, the location is said to be the highest point on the eastern seaboard south of Maine. From the observation deck of the light's north tower (a sixty-four-step climb), you see Sandy Hook, the Manhattan skyline, the ocean, and the coast of Long Island spread out like a giant map.

Built in 1862, the two brownstone light towers were once the most powerful lighthouses in the country and, in 1898, the first to be electrified. Though no longer in use, the New Jersey State Park Service maintains them for public viewing and, in conjunction with the Twin Lights Historical Society, operates a museum on the site. Here you will find a working replica of the equipment that Guglielmo Marconi used at Twin Lights in 1899 for the first-ever wireless telegraph transmission. Other exhibits include several locally built small boats and a superb collection of photos and equipment from the U.S. Lifesaving Service. Twin Lights is open year-round. Free admission.

◆ **FOR MORE INFORMATION:** Twin Lights Historic Site, P.O. Box 417, Highlands, NJ 07732; 908-872-1814.

BOAT TRIPS

Several party fishing boats operate out of the Sandy Hook Bay towns of Highlands and Atlantic Highlands. The *Sandy Hook Lady*, an eighty-five-foot stern-wheeler based at Atlantic Highlands Harbor, takes lunch, dinner, and sightseeing cruises through the bay and the nearby Navesink River. Prices range from $12 to $49.

Express Navigation's high-speed ferries to Manhattan also serve Highlands and Atlantic Highlands.

◆ **FOR MORE INFORMATION:**

Fishing: Atlantic Highlands Bait and Tackle Shop, 908-291-4500.

Sightseeing: *Sandy Hook Lady*, 908-291-4354.

Ferries: 800-BOATRIDE.

Old Barney and New Jersey's Mid-Coast

Barnegat Lighthouse is a Jersey Shore icon. The 172-foot-tall red-and-white tower, affectionately called "Old Barney" by everyone who has ever visited Long Beach Island, is one of the most photographed lighthouses in America. First lit in 1859, this lighthouse is also the best place to begin a visit to New Jersey's mid-coast. The panorama of shore towns, beaches, and bays that you see from the viewing area at the top of the tower is so rewarding that it makes the climb up a 217-step spiral staircase seem entirely worthwhile.

Look north across the inlet to see the Barnegat Peninsula (technically an island) with its combination of summer towns, active bay boating areas, amusement parks, beach boardwalks, and Island Beach State Park, a ten-mile-long protected sliver of sand and dunes.

POINT PLEASANT

Point Pleasant, the northernmost town on the Barnegat Peninsula, is also its most urban and offers good in-town shopping as well as a family-oriented boardwalk amusement area. The commercially operated Jenkinson's Beach is particularly popular and hosts a variety of summer entertainments, including weekly fireworks and laser shows. Several fishing party boats operate out of Point Pleasant, and the *River Belle*, an eighty-foot paddle-wheeler, offers lunch, dinner, and sightseeing cruises that travel through the Point Pleasant Canal to Barnegat Bay, passing beautiful bayfront homes along the way. On Thursday evenings, the *River Belle* runs a family "pizza-cruise" to watch the fireworks.

◆ FOR MORE INFORMATION:
River Belle, Broadway Basin, 47 Broadway, Point Pleasant Beach, NJ 08742; 908-892-3377.

Greater Point Pleasant Chamber of Commerce, 517A Arnold Avenue, Point Pleasant Beach, NJ 08742; 908-899-2424.

SEASIDE HEIGHTS

Seaside Heights, about twelve miles to the south, is the area's other hub of activity. Its oceanfront boardwalk has two piers of rides and games, making it a strong second to Wildwood as the shore's liveliest and biggest amusement center. If you prefer drive-yourself thrills, you can rent jet skis and other boats on Seaside's Barnegat Bay shore.

◆ **FOR MORE INFORMATION:** Seaside Heights Chamber of Commerce, Municipal Building, Box 32-R, Seaside Heights, NJ 08251; 908-793-9100.

BARNEGAT BAY

Barnegat Bay, New Jersey's largest bay, is a popular sailing spot, with an active yacht racing fleet. You can cruise on the bay aboard the *River Lady*, an eighty-five-foot paddle-wheeler that sails out of Toms River on the mainland side of the bay. To learn more about the bay's heritage, visit the small maritime museum run by the Toms River Seaport Society and the Barnegat Bay Decoy and Baymen's Museum in Tuckerton (see Chapter 2).

◆ **FOR MORE INFORMATION:** *River Lady*, 1 Robbins Parkway, Toms River, NJ 08754; 908-349-8664.

ISLAND BEACH STATE PARK

Arguably the best beach on the New Jersey coast, Island Beach State Park illustrates what the rest of the Barnegat Peninsula looked like before real estate developers and vacationers showed up. Apart from a few park buildings and some driftwood baymen's shacks, it is a wildlife area with an untouched dune ecosystem and a wonderful sandy beach for swimming, surfing, and fishing. Stop at the visitors center about a mile from the entrance to pick up maps, view exhibits, and walk along the self-guided nature trail that starts at the center. The park closes as soon as the 2,400-car parking area fills up, which assures an uncrowded beach, but one that is filled to capacity by 10:00 a.m. on nice summer days. The park is open year-round; there is a small per-car admission fee.

◆ **FOR MORE INFORMATION:** Island Beach State Park, Seaside Park, NJ 08752; 908-793-0506.

LONG BEACH ISLAND

Just a few hundred yards of water (but two bridges and seventy land miles) separate Island Beach from Barnegat Lighthouse, which sits at the northern tip of Long Beach Island (LBI), overlooking the entrance of Barnegat Inlet. Considered by many the most treacherous inlet north of Hatteras, Barnegat has constantly shifting shoals that have claimed many boats in bad weather.

But according to local legend, not all Jersey Shore shipwrecks can be attributed to natural phenomena. During the eighteenth century, Barnegat Pirates, as they were called, lured ships onto the shoals by hanging lanterns on mules and walking them slowly along the shore on moonless nights. Ship captains would assume the lights were other ships and head closer to shore for a better look. When the ploy worked and ships broke up on the shoals, the pirates had a heyday looting them.

Fortunately, LBI is a much friendlier place today. This nineteen-mile-long barrier island, which comprises Old Barney's southern view, is connected to the mainland by a two-mile causeway. The island, made up of a string of beach communities with colorful names — Ship Bottom, Harvey Cedars, Surf City, Loveladies, Beach Haven — is a popular family vacation spot.

BARNEGAT LIGHT

The towns of Barnegat Light at the north and Beach Haven near the southern end of the island have attractions of special note. Proximity to the inlet has made Barnegat Light (the town) an active fishing center, with many impressive-looking commercial boats and party boats that take visitors deep-sea fishing and sometimes whale watching.

The Barnegat Light Historical Museum (609-494-3407), located in a former one-room schoolhouse, displays the lighthouse's original lens as well as photographs and other local memorabilia. Open summer afternoons; a donation is requested.

BEACH HAVEN

Beach Haven is LBI's commercial hub, with a small museum, many restored Victorian buildings, restaurants, bed and breakfasts, and bayside facilities, where you can find sightseeing cruises and fishing trips. The Long Beach Island Historical Museum, located in an old Beach Haven church, has extensive exhibits depicting LBI's whaling and fishing days, a fascinating collection of photos of the 1962 storm that destroyed many island facilities, and special programs, including weekly walking tours.

The 100-foot, 300-passenger *Black Whale III* makes twice-daily casino excursions to Atlantic City. The ninety-minute (each way) cruise travels through the wetland areas of New Jersey's Intracoastal Waterway, and features live onboard entertainment, snacks, and a cash bar. Upon arrival in Atlantic City, passengers get a $15 coin bonus and seven hours on shore to see what they can win with it. Trips cost $30 per person. Its sister ship, *Black Whale II*, offers half-day fishing and evening bay cruises.

You will find boat rental places in several locations along the bay. The largest is Watersports, Inc., which has a variety of personal watercraft and crab boats for rent by the day or hour.

◆ FOR MORE INFORMATION:

LBI Historical Society, Engleside and Beach Avenues, Beach Haven, NJ 08008; 609-492-0700.

Black Whale II and *III*, Beach Haven Fishing Center, 450 Centre Street, Beach Haven, NJ 08008; 609-492-0333.

Watersports, Inc., 3100 Long Beach Boulevard, Brant Beach, NJ 08008; 609-494-2727.

Long Beach Island Chamber of Commerce, 265 West Ninth Street, Ship Bottom, NJ 08008; 609-494-7211.

Atlantic City

Atlantic City dominates New Jersey's coast, its neon glow visible from twenty miles north or south; its big-name entertainment, slot machines, and gaming tables drawing 30 million visitors each year; and its wide, easy-to-navigate inlet making it one of the most important commercial clam ports in the Northeast.

Clams are undoubtedly the last thing people think of when they visit Atlantic City, the home of America's first boardwalk and the Miss America Pageant, the birthplace of saltwater taffy, the inspiration for the game of Monopoly, and the East Coast's answer to a gambler's prayer. But for visitors with an interest in the sea, a side trip to the marina district near Harrah's and Trump Castle is a fascinating diversion.

Massive clam dredges — hefty ninety-foot boats with distinctive A-frame rigs — line the docks in Clam Creek, the large basin in front of Trump Castle. These vessels are responsible for bringing in the major portion of the U.S. catch of Atlantic surf clams and ocean quahogs, according to the National Marine Fisheries Service. These large clams — some have five-inch shells— are dredged up from the ocean floor many miles offshore, then loaded into cages on the boat and shipped to processing plants, where they are chopped up for chowder, clam strips, dips, and juices. It is impressive just to stand by the water and watch the fleet come back laden with thousands of pounds of clams.

You will get the best view of the area from the speedboat *Miss Atlantic City* (see Chapter 1), which gives a well-narrated tour of Clam Creek and nearby historic Gardner's Basin before it takes off for its high-speed thrill ride.

GARDNER'S BASIN

Gardner's Basin is a sheltered cove just off Absecon Inlet that was a favorite hiding place for seventeenth-century pirates, an important nineteenth-century whaling center, and a rum-running hub during Prohibition. It retains an authentically salty flavor thanks to active use by commercial clam and fishing boats, as well as year-round daily sailings of the *Captain Applegate*, a well-regarded party fishing boat. The Flying Cloud Restaurant (609-345-8222), a casual, moderately priced seafood restaurant with indoor and outdoor seating, and free docking for diners, is popular with salty locals.

A much-publicized effort to develop Gardner's Basin as a Mystic Seaport type of maritime village has thus far been unsuccessful, but the area comes alive during annual seafood and harbor festivals that bring thousands of visitors to the basin to sample a wide variety of food, crafts, and entertainment. Since the marina district is located in a tumbledown, out-of-the-way area of Atlantic City, it is best to travel there by cab.

ABSECON LIGHTHOUSE

Absecon Lighthouse stands 167 feet tall on the corner of Rhode Island and Pacific Avenues, a few blocks back from the sea. Built in 1857, it was designed by George Gordon Meade, who also designed Barnegat Lighthouse and later served as the Union commander at the Battle of Gettysburg. Unfortunately, the light has fallen victim to Atlantic City's uneven redevelopment. The neighborhood that surrounds it is run down and not recommended to tourists, and "Old Ab," which is no longer in use, is closed to the public. The best view of it, sad to say, is from the parking garage of the Showboat Casino Hotel.

Other highlights on a maritime tour of Atlantic City include the Atlantic City Coast Guard Station, a handsome 1941 Coast Guard building that houses a busy working station and is open for visits as part of the New Jersey Coastal Heritage Trail Program, and the Farley State Marina at Trump Castle, a great place for looking at luxury yachts and handsome sportfishing boats, some of which are available for charter.

◆ **FOR MORE INFORMATION:**

Miss Atlantic City, Farley State Marina, Atlantic City; mailing address: P.O. Box 20, Absecon, NJ 08201; 609-348-0800.

Captain Applegate, Gardner's Basin, Atlantic City, NJ 08401; 609-345-4077.

Atlantic City Coast Guard Station (located near Trump

Castle), 900 Beach Thoroughfare, Atlantic City, NJ 08401; 609-344-6594.

Senator Frank S. Farley State Marina, 600 Huron Avenue, Atlantic City, NJ 08401; 609-348-2292.

Wildwood and the Jersey Cape

From Ocean City with its boat parade and crustacean beauty contest to Wildwood with its boisterous boardwalk and adrenaline-pumping amusements, the Jersey Cape is a vacation playground that speaks to the kid in all of us. This "cape" is actually a series of Cape May County barrier islands with thirty miles of grand ocean beaches, boat-filled bays, and communities that court visitors with a never-ending series of summer programs and events.

OCEAN CITY

Ocean City, a former Methodist retreat and the Jersey Cape's only "dry" town, goes out of its way to prove that good times don't depend on wine and spirits. This distinctly family resort wins the prize for the most creative shore festivals: an annual baby parade, a hermit crab race, and one of New Jersey's most famous events, the annual Night in Venice Boat Parade, to name just a few. During Ocean City's Night in Venice, held each July, a hundred or more lavishly decorated boats — from yachts to kayaks — parade through the lagoons. Ocean City's two-mile-long boardwalk has rides and games geared primarily to children and young teens, and a Music Pier where you can hear live music, ranging from classical to rock, nearly every summer night.

◆ **FOR MORE INFORMATION:** Ocean City Public Relations Department, 9th Street and Asbury Avenue, Ocean City, NJ 08226; 609-525-9300 or 800-BEACH-NJ.

WILDWOOD

Wildwood, the shore's best-known amusement area, is a no-holds-barred oceanside carnival with one of the biggest and best beaches on the shore (and one of the few that is free). Two piers offer over a hundred stomach-twisting theme-park-quality thrill rides, including a looping roller coaster that does half the trip backward. At night, the piers — Morey's Pier and Mariner's Landing — are a blur of colors, squeals, and irresistible junk food smells, an atmosphere that's heaven to teens and twenty-somethings, who flock there by the thousands. Wildwood can be noisy, crowded, and a bit raucous. But the piers are clean and well run, and judging by the smiles one sees everywhere, the festive hubbub has appeal to people of all ages. For daytime thrills, Morey's also runs Raging Waters, a two-site oceanside water park with twisting water slides and simulated rivers for whitewater tubing.

◆ **FOR MORE INFORMATION:** Wildwood Department of Tourism, Box 609, Boardwalk and Schellenger Avenue, Wildwood, NJ 08260; 609-522-1407 or 800-WW-BY-SEA.

BEACH COMMUNITIES

By contrast, Sea Isle City, Avalon, and Stone Harbor are relatively quiet communities where pristine beaches and beautiful dunes are the prime attraction. Sea Isle City is also famous for its

A waverunner at Wildwood Shore, New Jersey

fleet of party fishing boats, which leave the docks daily for four-, six- or eight-hour fishing trips. Stone Harbor is home to a heron rookery where visitors can see thousands of shorebirds every day, and the Wetlands Institute, an environmental research laboratory with a popular nature center (see Chapter 7).

◆ **FOR MORE INFORMATION:** Cape May County Chamber of Commerce, Cape May Court House, NJ 08210; 609-465-7181.

HEREFORD INLET LIGHTHOUSE

To learn something about the history of the Wildwood area, visit the Hereford Inlet Lighthouse, a pretty two-story Victorian house with a light tower on top, which overlooks the once-busy inlet in the Anglesea area of North Wildwood. Now listed on the National Register of Historic Places, the 1874-vintage light survived the battering of many ocean storms, but was almost lost to neglect after the U.S. Coast Guard decommissioned it in the 1960s. Local citizens soon rallied to the cause, however, restoring the lighthouse and opening it to visitors in 1984. Two years later, the Coast Guard relit its lantern and reactivated it as an aid to navigation. The lighthouse, which is open from June until September, displays a collection of photographs and artifacts of the Anglesea area and is also the site of concerts and outdoor festivals.

◆ **FOR MORE INFORMATION:** Hereford Lighthouse Restoration, P.O. Box 499, North Wildwood, NJ 08260; 609-522-4520.

BOAT RIDES

Cape May County remains an active boating area and offers more rental and passenger boats per mile of shorefront than any other area of the New Jersey coast. Drive along the bayshore in almost any community and you will find opportunities for on-the-water adventure that rival the boardwalk thrill rides, including parasailing, jet ski and personal watercraft rentals, speedboats, offshore fishing trips, whale and dolphin watching excursions, and sightseeing cruises. Travelers' tip: Many companies offer discounts, so look for coupons in local newspapers and visitors centers. The following are some of the many boating possibilities:

Big Flamingo, Sinn's Dock, 6006 Park Boulevard, Wildwood Crest; 609-522-3934. Sightseeing, whale and dolphin watching trips.

Captain Schumann's *Big Blue Sightseer*, 4500 Park Boulevard, Wildwood; 609-522-2919. Wildwood and Cape May cruises, marine mammal watching trips on an eighty-foot converted World War II PT boat. Captain Charles Schumann, who works as a commercial fisherman in the off-season, is a favorite with local environmental groups because of the respectful way he operates the boat around whales and dolphin.

Delta Lady, Wildwood Marina, Rio Grande and Susquehanna Avenues, Wildwood; 609-522-1919. Narrated inland waterway tours on a Mississippi River–style paddle-wheeler.

North Star and *Evening Star*, Palen Avenue, Ocean City; 609-399-7588. Sightseeing cruises with commentary on historic sights and marine life aboard a fishing party boat that cruises Ocean City's coast.

Parasailing Adventures, Ocean Drive, Wildwood Crest; 609-522-1869. Tours of Cape May and Wildwood beaches from 300 or 600 feet above the water in a speedboat-towed parachute.

Princess Cruises, City Marina, 42nd Street and the Bay, Sea Isle City; 609-263-1633 Evening music cruises; daytime sightseeing and dolphin watch trips.

Starlight Fleet, Blake's Dock, 6200 Park Boulevard, Wildwood Crest; 609-729-7776. Sunset sightseeing cruises of Cape May and Wildwood area, dolphin watch trips and evening party cruises with DJ.

And don't forget the great Jersey Shore speedboats *Flying Saucer, PT-109,* and *Silver Bullet*, described in Chapter 1.

Cape May
Cape May, New Jersey's southernmost city, bills itself as America's oldest seashore resort — the place where the Lenni Lenape Indians came to fish and enjoy cool ocean breezes before

Europeans ever landed on American soil, and where early colonists went to experience the benefits of ocean bathing.

But it was as a nineteenth-century resort that Cape May flourished, attracting wealthy vacationers from New York, Washington, and Philadelphia who built stunning homes, many of which have been restored and preserved in elegant detail. Over 600 Victorian structures remain (several of which are now bed and breakfasts), lending Cape May a genteel old-world charm and earning the entire city designation as a National Historic Landmark.

As it has been for centuries, the sea is Cape May's chief attraction. Once an island, the city is now a peninsula with the Atlantic Ocean on its eastern shore and Delaware Bay on the west. It has a vast expanse of clean and popular swimming beaches, a sheltered harbor, and an extensive area of salt marshes. Cape May's location on the Atlantic Flyway makes it one of the premier locations for observing birds in North America.

The shoreline surrounding Cape May Harbor is a thriving maritime area with wharves for oceangoing commercial fishing boats to unload their catch, and docks where passengers can board boats for sightseeing, fishing, and whale/dolphin watching excursions. Fisherman's Wharf and the docks surrounding the popular Lobster House restaurant provide a great vantage point for watching the activity. The Lobster House (609-884-8296) is an attraction in itself, with its outdoor raw bar, dining area on the deck of a historic schooner, indoor dining rooms, and large fish market.

Boat tours of Cape May travel past the fishing docks, through wildlife-rich inland waterway areas, past Victorian homes, and through the Cape May Canal — built during World War II to give navy ships safe passage from Delaware Bay to the ocean without facing danger from enemy submarines near Cape May Point. Once past the point, you are likely to see bottlenose dolphin and perhaps whales in ocean waters. Because of this latter possibility, many of the companies advertise these tours as whale watches (see Chapter 7 for additional information). Boats depart from docks near the Cape May Canal. Note, also, that some boats operating out of nearby Wildwood also offer Cape May tours. Call ahead for schedule and price information.

Cape May Whale Watcher, Second Avenue and Wilson Drive, Cape May, NJ 08240; 609-884-5445

Cape May Whale Watch and Research Center, 1286 Wilson Drive, Cape May, NJ 08240; 609-898-0055

Miss Chris Fishing Boats, Third Avenue and Wilson Drive, Cape May, NJ 08204; 609-884-3939

Schooner *Yankee* (see Chapter 1), Ocean Highway Docks, Cape May, NJ 08204; 609-884-1919

Shore Shot (speedboat, see Chapter 1), Miss Chris Fishing Center, Third Avenue and Wilson Drive, Cape May, NJ 08204; 609-886-6161.

Sunset Dinner and Dolphin Cruise, Utsch's Marina, Highway 109, Cape May, NJ 08024; 609-898-0999.

The Cape May–Lewes Ferry, a large car-carrying vessel, crosses Delaware Bay, linking the New Jersey and Delaware coasts. It offers an $8.50 round-trip "foot excursion" special that includes a seventy-minute cruise across the bay and free bus transportation to key sights in either port; 800-64-FERRY.

MID-ATLANTIC CENTER FOR THE ARTS

The Mid-Atlantic Center for the Arts (known locally as MAC) is a Cape May visitor's best friend. This not-for-profit group spearheaded the city's successful 1970s preservation movement and now manages several historic sites. MAC sponsors an amazingly diverse selection of regularly scheduled tours and special events, including tours of the fishing wharves, special narrated boat trips, mansion tours, concerts, and special programs at the Cape May Lighthouse.

CAPE MAY LIGHTHOUSE

Cape May Lighthouse, located in Cape May Point State Park about two miles southwest of the center of town, overlooks the entrance of Delaware Bay. This 157-foot tower, built in 1859, is another of the oldest continually operating lighthouses in the United States. For a spectacular view of the coast, climb the 199-step cast-iron spiral staircase to the visitors gallery just below the lantern. Note the concrete bunker on the beach below, built during World War II as part of the U.S. coastal defense network, and be sure to look for dolphin swimming in the nearby waters. Visitors not up to the climb can see a photo mural of the view and a video about the lighthouse in the adjacent MAC-operated museum and visitors center. Admission: $3.50 for adults; $1 for children.

◆ **FOR MORE INFORMATION:**

Mid-Atlantic Center for the Arts, 1048 Washington Street, P.O. Box 340, Cape May, NJ 08204; 609-884-5404.

Cape May Lighthouse; 609-884-8656.

Cape May Point State Park, P.O. Box 107, Cape May Point, NJ 08212; 609-884-2159.

Cape May County Chamber of Commerce, Cape May Court House, NJ 08210; 609-465-7181.

The Delsea Region

The Delsea region, as New Jersey's southwest coast is called, is the kind of place where you find crabs crossing the road, and locals who stop whatever they are doing to pick them up and toss them back into the bay. After a couple of hours in Bivalve or Shellpile, one views the act as completely in character.

For centuries these towns and others like them along the Maurice (pronounced Morris) River and Delaware Bay have depended on the sea for their livelihood. In fact, until the 1950s when a parasite known as MSX showed up, the area was one of the world's premier oyster ports, where millions of pounds of oysters were harvested, processed, and shipped annually. Today, the oyster boats sit at the docks waiting for a healthy harvest, which, researchers predict, may come soon. Meanwhile, crabbing has become a principal industry.

Located in Cumberland County less than an hour's drive from Cape May County's ocean beaches, New Jersey's Delaware Bay coast offers a refreshing change from the bustling boardwalks of the east. Here you will find mile upon mile of protected marshes and wetlands, nearly empty bay beaches, and communities with seafaring pasts struggling to keep marine businesses alive.

Thus far, the area is remarkably untouristy, which gives it great charm, but makes it a challenge to explore. Roads are poorly marked, and there are few guidebooks. That may change before long, however. Local merchants and community leaders are hoping that "eco-tourism" will give the Delsea region an economic boost, and they are talking about setting up interpretive centers that will make it easier for visitors to enjoy the region's natural beauty. The following are three locations of special maritime interest.

EAST POINT LIGHTHOUSE

Located in the marshes near the entrance of the Maurice River, East Point Lighthouse is the last remaining lighthouse on the shore of Delaware Bay. Built in 1849 and commissioned in 1852, the now-automated lantern is housed in a bright red cupola that sits atop a two-and-a-half-story brick house. The all-volunteer Maurice River Historical Society maintains the lighthouse and is hoping to raise half a million dollars to restore the interior and open it as a museum. At present, visitors can go inside only during a special open house, usually held the first week of August, but you can visit the grounds any time. Follow the signs for East Point, near Heislerville on NJ Route 47.

◆ **FOR MORE INFORMATION:** Maurice River Historical Society, c/o Jim Gowdy, P.O. Box 175, Mizpah, NJ 08342; 609-476-4532.

DELAWARE BAY SCHOONER PROJECT

The Delaware Bay Schooner Project, a grassroots not-for-profit organization founded in 1988, is an active protector and promoter of Delaware Bay maritime traditions. Under the direction of its energetic and dedicated founder, Meghan Wren, the Schooner Project has raised close to $600,000 for the authentic reconstruction of the oyster schooner *A. J. Meerwald/Clyde A. Phillips*, which will begin taking the public on education-oriented sails in late 1995 or early 1996 (see Chapter 1). The Schooner Project maintains a visitors center in a storefront in Port Norris, sponsors an annual Delaware Bay celebration, hosts maritime lectures, and eventually hopes to restore a section of the original Maurice River Shipping Sheds, which it purchased in 1994. Public participation is always welcome and encouraged.

◆ **FOR MORE INFORMATION:** Delaware Bay Schooner Project, P.O. Box 57, Dorchester, NJ 08316; 609-785-2060.

FORTESCU STATE MARINA

Once known as the "Weakfish Capital of the World," Fortescue State Marina is a third local point of interest. Although weakfish are no longer plentiful, Fortescue (south of the town of Newport off County Road 553) remains the hub of Delaware Bay recreational fishing. Several party and charter boats offer half- or full-day fishing trips, and some captains recently began running occasional tours of the Delaware Bay shoal lighthouses.

◆ **FOR MORE INFORMATION:** Fortescue Captains and Boat Owners Association; 609-447-5115.

The Delsea region lends itself to leisurely meandering and unexpected discoveries: an empty beach, a pretty town (don't miss Mauricetown, an old sea captains' village with many beautiful homes), a fisherman who will spin tales of oystering days, a small boat to rent for touring or crabbing, or a volunteer fireman who wants to sell you a ticket to one of the area's traditional ham and oyster suppers. Buy it, and experience the hospitality of a still unspoiled region of New Jersey's coast.

New Jersey Coastal Heritage Trail

As you tour New Jersey shore areas, look for signs marking points of interest along the newly established New Jersey Coastal Heritage Trail (NJCHT). A joint effort by the National Park Service, the State of New Jersey, and many coastal organizations, its goal is to preserve and promote the natural and cultural heritage of shore areas. Eventually, several welcome centers will provide literature that highlights five coastal themes: coastal communities, shoreside relaxation and inspiration, maritime history, wildlife migration, and coastal habitats. In 1993, some interim welcome centers opened and the first trail markers went up, directing people to sites that have significance in maritime history, including lighthouses, Coast Guard Stations, marinas, and museums. Several locations described in this chapter already sport NJCHT signs.

◆ **FOR MORE INFORMATION:** New Jersey Coastal Heritage Trail, P.O. Box 118, Mauricetown, NJ 08329; 609-785-0676.

New Jersey's Travel and Tourism office publishes several excellent guides to places of interest in the state. These include a guide to cultural institutions, a comprehensive calendar of events, and travel guides to local areas.

◆ **FOR MORE INFORMATION:** New Jersey Division of Travel and Tourism, CN 826, Trenton, NJ 08625; 609-292-2470 or 800-JERSEY-7.

◆ 4 ◆
The Hudson River

"Heave away, Haul away, Heave ..." The giant mainsail of the Hudson River Sloop *Clearwater* inches up the mast as we haul the halyard, hand-over-hand, to the rhythmic cadence of a sea chantey. I am lost in time, repeating a ritual that dates back two centuries to the days when cargo and passenger sloops crowded the Hudson River.

"That's it. Drop the line," the crew chief calls. Beside me, forty-five fourth graders smile broadly as the wind fills the sail and the sloop heels gently. As part of *Clearwater*'s volunteer crew, it's my job to teach these youngsters something about the wonders of the Hudson River.

The *Clearwater,* a 106-foot replica of the sloops that sailed on the Hudson during the eighteenth and nineteenth centuries, is the quintessential Hudson River boat, representing the traditions of the past as well as the hope for the river's future. The brainchild of folksinger and activist Pete Seeger, who believed that a beautiful sloop would inspire public action to improve the river and its ecology, the fifty-passenger *Clearwater* celebrated its twenty-fifth birthday in 1994 and has been largely successful in achieving its goals. The river is now cleaner and healthier than it has been in decades.

The Hudson, which winds through New York State like a deep blue ribbon for 315 miles from its source in the Adirondacks to its mouth in New York Harbor, is a river of contrasts. It flows through farmland and between mountain ranges, past quaint towns and beside bustling cities. It is, geologists say, a fjord, like those of Norway, carved by glacial erosion and flooded by the sea. It is also one of the richest estuaries on the East Coast.

Discovered in 1524 by Giovanni da Verrazano, who described it as "an exceeding great stream of water," the Hudson River was first explored eighty-five years later by Henry Hudson, who, thinking he'd found the Northwest Passage to China, sailed the *Half Moon* north to the end of navigable water at Albany. Almost immediately, the river became an important commercial route as sturdy sloops brought cargo to and from the north. In 1825, when the Erie Canal opened, the Hudson became New York's link with the West.

There are many ways to experience the Hudson's history, rich natural resources, and stunning scenic beauty. Roads leading to shoreside attractions parallel both sides of the river, and many places are accessible by bus or train. Sightseeing and dining cruises sail from a number of river towns. Several groups, most notably the Shorewalkers (212-330-7686) and the Appalachian Mountain Club (212-986-1430), currently lead walks along the shore and hikes to the summits of nearby mountains where the view can be savored from above.

Riverfront access improves each year, and ten years from now, according to a plan authorized by the New York State Legislature in 1991, you should be able to walk beside the river on the Hudson River Greenway Trail all the way from the tip of Manhattan to Cohoes, about 155 miles to the north.

Touring by Boat

You can admire the Hudson from many vantage points, but if you want to enjoy and experience the river itself, treat yourself to a boat ride. Smell the air (salty from New York Harbor to Poughkeepsie), hear the chug of tugboats pushing oil barges, get close to lighthouses, pass beneath the bridges, watch the ever-changing sky, and take in the panorama of rock cliffs and misty hills, so beautiful they inspired America's first school of landscape painting, the nineteenth-century Hudson River School. The view is particularly spectacular in autumn when swatches of crimson from Virginia creeper and streaks of gold and yellow from wild grapes thread the hills, and the maples, hickories, and oaks turn vibrant shades of red, orange, and russet.

From the day in 1807 when Robert Fulton steamed upriver aboard the *Clermont,* for the first successful steamboat ride ever, the Hudson has been a popular cruising ground. Although the glorious steamers are gone, comfortable tour boats still offer overnight cruises between New York City and Albany, as well as short sightseeing cruises from a number of different locations. It is also possible to spend a week or an hour in a sailboat on the river.

Except for special canal lock tours, most passenger vessels don't sail above Troy, where the river joins the Champlain Canal for forty miles. In its northernmost reaches, the Hudson is a wild and often turbulent mountain stream, navigable only by extremely skillful whitewater canoeists and rafters. Most boats operate from May through October, and prices listed are actual 1994 rates; most operators said they anticipated little or no change in future years.

Sailing Vessels

The Hudson River Sloop *Clearwater* is a boat with a mission. Sailings on this 106-foot replica of eighteenth-century river sloops are all educational outings for school and adult civic groups that leave from different locations on the Hudson River, New York Harbor, New Jersey, and Long Island Sound. Everyone aboard participates in raising the one-ton mainsail, singing chanteys, catching fish, learning about Hudson River history and ecology, and even taking the tiller. The *Clearwater* has no public pay-as-you-go sailing program, but *Clearwater* members ($25 for individuals; $35 for families) can participate in member sails for a nominal fee. Members can also apply to sail for a week as volunteer crew (no experience necessary). The only cost is a $35 contribution for the week's meals (hearty, mostly vegetarian fare). If you don't mind hard work and communal living, it's a great way to spend a week on the water.

◆ **FOR MORE INFORMATION:** Hudson River Sloop *Clearwater,* Inc., 112 Market Sreet, Poughkeepsie, NY 12601; 914-454-7673.

The *Woody Guthrie,* a thirty-two-foot gaff-rigged ferry sloop with tanbark sails, is Pete Seeger's second gift to the Hudson River community. Seeger and his wife, Toshi, commissioned the boat, which is modeled after the ferryboats that carried passengers from town to town during the 1800s. The Seegers then donated it to the not-for-profit Beacon Sloop Club, on the condition that club members take people sailing and teach them about the river. Up to twelve guests can sail for free on evenings and weekends from May to November. The *Guthrie,* which looks like a miniature *Clearwater,* departs from Beacon's Hudson River pier. Sailings are open to anyone who calls and reserves a space. Beacon Sloop Club members ($10 annual fee) can also participate in a small-boat sailing program.

◆ **FOR MORE INFORMATION:** Beacon Sloop Club, P.O. Box 527, Beacon, NY 12508; 914-561-7726.

Sojourner Truth, a thirty-two-foot ferro-cement ferry sloop, built and maintained by volunteers, has been sailing out of Yonkers, New York, since 1983. Named for a former slave who made her first trip as a free woman on a ferry sloop in the early nineteenth century, *Sojourner Truth* belongs to an environmental organization called Ferry Sloops, which sponsors both environmental education and sail training programs. Members ($20 for individuals; $30 for households) sail on the *Sojourner Truth* for free.

◆ **FOR MORE INFORMATION:** Ferry Sloops, 3 JFK Memorial Drive, Yonkers, NY 10701; 914-376-0906.

Sailboat Rentals and Lessons

Myles Gordon's Great Hudson Sailing Center gives sailing lessons and rents sailboats from sixteen to forty-three feet (with and without captains) from Haverstraw Bay, nine miles north of the Tappan Zee Bridge, and from Kingston's Rondout Creek. Rentals start at $200 per day. The New York/North Jersey Chapter of the Appalachian Mountain Club also organizes low-cost sailing outings and instruction from several river locations, and SEAS Westchester, an affiliate of the Society for the Education of American Sailors, operates a sailing club and offers low-cost instruction in cooperation with the American Red Cross from Tarrytown.

◆ **FOR MORE INFORMATION:**

Great Hudson Sailing Center, Main Office, Haverstraw Marina, Beach Road, Haverstraw, NY 10993; 914-429-1557.

Appalachian Mountain Club, 202 East 39th Street, New York, NY 10016; 212-986-1430.

SEAS Westchester, P.O. Box 892, White Plains, NY 10602; 914-631-4164.

Sightseeing Cruises

New York Waterway, the enterprising private ferry company that almost single-handedly brought about a resurgence in New York Harbor ferry transit during the 1980s, launched its Historic Hudson cruise in 1993. The ferry departs mornings from Weehawken, New Jersey, and West 38th Street in Manhattan for a ninety-minute narrated cruise to Tarrytown, twenty-five miles upriver. There, passengers have a choice of two tours. The Sleepy Hollow tour includes visits to Philipsburg Manor, a restored eighteenth-century farm, and to Sunnyside, the home of author Washington Irving, whose tales of Rip Van Winkle and Ichabod Crane are Hudson River legends. The other tour explores Kykuit, the palatial Rockefeller estate, which was opened to the public for the first time in 1994. The boat returns in late afternoon. Snack bar onboard. Tickets, which include the round-trip boat ride and admission to the historic sites, are $35 for the Sleepy Hollow Tour,

$50 for Kykuit. Beginning in 1995, New York Waterway will run two-day trips to these Tarrytown attractions that include meals and a stay at an upscale hotel.

◆ **FOR MORE INFORMATION:** New York Waterway, Pershing Road, Weehawken, NJ 07087; 800-533-3779.

Express Navigation, which operates rush-hour commuter ferry service between New Jersey and New York aboard luxurious high-speed catamarans, puts the boats to work on fall weekends with narrated Hudson River cruises during the height of the foliage season and trips to West Point for Army football games. Boats depart from Atlantic Highlands, New Jersey. Sightseeing tickets include lunch at a riverside restaurant, and the football excursion includes a game ticket. Each is priced at $50. Full bar onboard.

◆ **FOR MORE INFORMATION:** Express Navigation, 2 First Avenue, Atlantic Highlands, NJ 07716; 800-BOATRIDE (800-262-8743).

Hudson Highlands Cruises and Tours, Inc., offers narrated sightseeing cruises on the M/V *Commander,* a historic seventy-foot/one-hundred-passenger ferryboat built in 1917 and listed on the National and State Registers of Historic Places. Two options are available: Passengers can board at Haverstraw for a six-and-a-half-hour cruise that includes a two-hour stop at West Point or they can take a one-and-a-half-hour lunchtime cruise from the West Point dock. Highlights include views of the Stony Point Lighthouse and Battlefield; Bear Mountain State Park; the towns of Garrison and Cold Spring; Bannerman's Island with its ruined castle, built in the early 1900s by a munitions dealer who used it to store arms; and Storm King Mountain, one of the river's most spectacular natural landmarks. Snack bar and full liquor bar onboard. Tickets: $9 to $16.

◆ **FOR MORE INFORMATION:** Hudson Highlands Cruises and Tours, Inc., P.O. Box 265, Highland Falls, NY 10928; 914-446-7171.

The not-for-profit **Constitution Island Association** runs tours from West Point on Wednesdays and Thursdays during the summer months. A forty-passenger military launch makes the fifteen-minute trip through the narrowest and deepest stretch of the Hudson to Constitution Island, an important Revolutionary War outpost. The guided tour of the island includes the Warner House, an early-nineteenth-century home with beautiful gardens, and a visit to the site where a great chain was stretched across the river to block British passage during the Revolutionary War. (You can see links of the actual chain at West Point.) Tickets: $7 adults; $6 children and seniors.

◆ **FOR MORE INFORMATION:** Constitution Island Association, P.O. Box 41, West Point, NY 10966; 914-446-8676.

Pride of the Hudson, a 149-passenger sightseeing boat, sails south through the Highlands from Newburgh, New York. The two-hour narrated cruise passes Beacon, Storm King Mountain, and Bannerman's Island, and offers a glimpse of West Point in the distance. Evening music cruises feature special party themes. Tickets: $9 and up. Bar onboard.

◆ **FOR MORE INFORMATION:** Hudson River Adventures, Inc., R.D. 3, Box 809, Monroe, NY 10959; 914-782-0685.

River Queen, a double-deck paddle-wheeler licensed for 149 passengers, offers sightseeing, brunch, dinner, dancing, and entertainment cruises from Poughkeepsie. Hudson River mansions, the Esopus Lighthouse, and the foothills of the Catskill Mountains are highlights. Tickets: $10 to $28; kids and seniors less.

◆ **FOR MORE INFORMATION:** Riverboat Tours, 310 Mill Street, Poughkeepsie, NY 12601; 914-473-5211.

Departing from Kingston's historic Rondout Creek, M/V *Rip Van Winkle* offers two-hour scenic cruises, day-long trips to West Point, and evening music cruises with a live band. Two-hour cruises sail through the Catskill area, past Victorian homes, the

Roosevelt and Vanderbilt mansions, and two lighthouses — Esopus Meadows and Rondout II. The all-day cruise adds the spectacular scenery of the Highlands as well. Owner/captain Jerry Henne is famous for his colorful narration. Ask him to tell you about the island that was towed down from Maine. Tickets $12 to $20; kids and seniors less. Bar and deli onboard. Henne's company also runs trips from the Hudson River Maritime Museum to the Rondout II Lighthouse.

◆ **FOR MORE INFORMATION:** Hudson River Cruises, Inc., P.O. Box 333, Rifton, NY 12471; 914-255-6515.

North River Cruises' motor yacht *Teal* also offers customized sightseeing and dinner cruises departing from Kingston's Rondout Creek. Owner/captain John Cutten operates his business with an emphasis on elegance. Prices vary, depending on the cruise or event. In the autumn, River Valley Tours, Inc., uses the *Teal* for week-long cruises between Troy and New York City. Passengers are bused to shoreside attractions and dine and spend the night at Hudson River Valley inns. The price is $1,495 per person.

◆ **FOR MORE INFORMATION:**

North River Cruises, 24 Cutten Drive, Saugerties, NY 12477; 914-679-8205.

River Valley Tours, Inc. P.O. Box 743, New Paltz, NY 12561; 800-836-2128.

Operating out of the Port of Albany, *Dutch Apple II* offers two-hour sightseeing cruises of the upper Hudson that pass by rolling hills, Dutch houses, grand mansions, and Albany's commercial waterfront and Capital buildings. Other trips include lunch and dinner/dance cruises, cruises to the Troy lock, and a two-day bus-and-boat tour from Albany to New York City. Onboard bar. Tickets: $9 to $28 for day trips, kids less; overnight cruise, $259 per person.

◆ **FOR MORE INFORMATION:** Dutch Apple Cruises, P.O. Box 395, Albany, NY; 518-463-0220.

The *Spirit of St. Joseph*, a 200-passenger stern-wheeler operating out of Rensselaer, which bills itself as "the friendliest cruise boat on the Hudson River," is a mom-and-pop operation in the best sense of the phrase. Peg Montepare is the captain, and her husband Joe the band leader. Together they offer an eclectic selection of regularly scheduled river cruises, ranging from senior citizen luncheons and 1950s music cruises to family sightseeing excursions around New York's Capital District and special lock tours. Onboard bar and snack bar. Tickets: $8 to $16.95. Two-day cruises from Albany to New York City take place in the fall ($199 per person).

◆ **FOR MORE INFORMATION:** Pegasus Riverboat Company, Inc., 40 Riverside Avenue, Rensselaer, NY; 518-449-2664 or 800-828-2364.

Captain J.P., a three-deck, 110-foot paddle-wheeler, brings Mississippi showboat traditions to the restored waterfront of the City of Troy with a series of themed entertainment cruises, as well as lunch, dinner, and sightseeing trips. Highlights include the Albany skyline, the Troy dam and lock at the beginning of the New York State Canal System, and pastoral river landscapes. The *Captain J.P.* also runs two-day bus-and-boat excursions to New York City. Tickets: $5.95 to $210 (for the two-day trip).

◆ **FOR MORE INFORMATION:** *Captain J.P.* Cruise Lines, 278 River Street, Troy, NY 12180; 518-270-1901.

The **American/Canadian/Caribbean Line** and the **Clipper Cruise Line** sail through the Hudson River as part of their fall foliage cruises, offering good food, comfortable onboard accommodations, and lectures about the history and scenic attractions of the area (see Chapter 1).

Lighthouses and Landmarks

When they were built during the nineteenth and early twentieth centuries, the Hudson River lighthouses were beacons that guided riverboats and ships past the shoals that line the river's shores. Today they shine as examples of the loving hard work of local preservationists who raised funds and/or battled government agencies to save these historic structures from decay and certain demolition. Of the seven that remain, four are open to the public, with one — the Saugerties Light — providing overnight guest accommodations.

Jeffrey's Hook, the fat red light beneath the George Washington Bridge depicted in the 1942 children's book *The Little Red Lighthouse and the Great Gray Bridge*, was erected on the Manhattan side of the Hudson in 1921, and slated for demolition in 1951. Contrary to the popular story, the bright bridge lights made Little Red's beacon obsolete, but public outcry saved the structure, which is now owned by the New York City Parks Department. The best way to see the light and the only way to go inside is to join one of the Urban Park Rangers' free tours held periodically during the summer months.

◆ **FOR MORE INFORMATION:** NYC Urban Park Rangers, 1234 Fifth Avenue, New York, NY; 718-383-6363.

The spark-plug-shaped **Tarrytown Lighthouse**, built in 1883 and located in Kingsland Point Park in Tarrytown, is one of several Hudson River lighthouses that were "family stations," with living quarters inside the lighthouse structure. You can climb to the top of this sixty-foot light, view the simple furnishings, and see photos and copies of the keepers' logs during free tours conducted periodically by the Hudson River Foundation in cooperation with the Westchester County Department of Parks, Recreation and Preservation.

◆ **FOR MORE INFORMATION:** Westchester County Parks Administration, 19 Bradhurst Avenue, Hawthorne, NY 10532; 914-831-1641.

Stony Point Lighthouse, an octagonal stone tower located 150 feet above the west side of the river, dates from 1825 and is the Hudson's oldest lighthouse. It is not currently open to the public, but the Palisades Interstate Park Commission, which owns and maintains the light as part of the Stony Point Battlefield Historic Site, hopes to raise funds for renovation. The battlefield, where "Mad Anthony" Wayne and 1,200 Continentals stormed and captured a British fort in July 1779, is worth a visit on its own.

◆ **FOR MORE INFORMATION:** Stony Point Battlefield and Museum, Park Road, Stony Point, NY 10980; 914-786-2521.

The gothic towers of the United States Military Academy at **West Point** are the Hudson's most dramatic landmark. Highlights are a museum with one of the world's best collections of military memorabilia and firearms, the Cadet Chapel with the largest church organ in the world, cadet parades, and football games. My own favorite spot is Trophy Point, where you can see links of the 150-ton, 600-yard iron chain that blocked the river during the Revolutionary War and enjoy one of the best river views in the Hudson Highlands. Bus and self-guided walking tours are available.

◆ **FOR MORE INFORMATION:** United States Military Academy Visitors Center, Route 9W, West Point, NY 10966; 914-938-2517.

Rondout II Lighthouse, located on a man-made island near the entrance of Rondout Creek, offers a real glimpse of lighthouse living. The lantern tower is attached to a comfortable three-story brick house, where lighthouse keepers and their families lived from 1913 until the 1960s. Authentic furnishings, complete with dishes and kitchen utensils, give Rondout II a homey feel, and photos and keepers' logs depict life at the light. The view from the tower is grand. The now-automated light is operated as a navigational aid by the U.S. Coast Guard; the Hudson River Maritime Museum maintains the building and artifacts. A ten-minute ride on the *Indy 7*, a forty-foot open launch that was once a liberty boat for the aircraft carrier USS *Independence,* will take you there from either side of the river. The boat operates from the Hudson River Maritime Museum in Kingston and from Rhinecliff Landing near the railroad station on the east side of the river. Tickets, which

Catching the Hudson River Spirit

"The protection of the environment is as important a part of our Hudson River culture as fishermen, orchards, vineyards, and the Revolutionary War," says John Cronin, the official Hudson Riverkeeper, who spends his life patrolling the river in a small boat and taking action (in the courts when necessary) to stop those he catches polluting. He is something of a local legend, the subject of a children's book and several articles, but he is only one of the people who put passion to work for the Hudson River.

These river lovers, who belong to a number of different groups, sponsor river festivals and other events throughout the year, all of which make wonderful ways for visitors to catch the Hudson River spirit. Most events feature food, music, displays of local culture and history, and friendly people who love sharing river stories.

You'll find a shadfest, sponsored by a local group and the Hudson River Foundation, almost every weekend day during May at some river town. There you'll taste baked, smoked, and potted shad — for free — and learn about one of the richest fishing traditions on the Hudson.

The *Clearwater*, regarded as the flagship of the environmental movement, sponsors a two-day fair and concert every June, called Clearwater's Hudson River Revival. During the annual *Clearwater* Pumpkin Sail in October, the sloop brings music-makers and pumpkins to towns along the river.

◆ **FOR MORE INFORMATION:** Hudson River Foundation, 20 West 20th Street, New York, NY 10011; 212-924-8290.

Hudson River Sloop *Clearwater*, Inc., 112 Market Street, Poughkeepsie, NY 12601; 914-454-7673.

include the boat ride, lighthouse tour, and museum admission, are $5 (children under four free). See Chapter 2 for a description of the Hudson River Maritime Museum, a not-to-be-missed Hudson River attraction.

◆ **FOR MORE INFORMATION:** Hudson River Maritime Museum, 1 Rondout Landing, Kingston, NY 12401; 914-338-0071.

When the not-for-profit Saugerties Lighthouse Conservancy acquired the **Saugerties Lighthouse** in 1986, it wasn't much more than a loose pile of bricks ready to fall into the river. After an elaborate (mostly volunteer) reconstruction project, the light was restored to operation in 1990, and the structure, a "family" lighthouse that dates to 1867, was opened to visitors in 1991. In addi-

Saugerties Lighthouse on the Hudson

tion to the living quarters — where you can stay overnight ($75 for a double) — you'll see models, photos, a video of the lighthouse restoration, and memorabilia from Saugerties's nineteenth-century steamship days. The lighthouse is about a half-mile walk over a sometimes soggy path from a parking lot adjacent to the Esopus Creek Coast Guard Station. Open weekends during summer and fall.

◆ **FOR MORE INFORMATION:** Saugerties Lighthouse Conservancy, 914-786-2521.

Local preservation groups are currently restoring the two remaining Hudson River lighthouses, Esopus Meadows (914-338-4090) and Hudson-Athens (518-828-3828). They are not yet open to visitors, but volunteers and donors are welcome.

◆ 5 ◆
The Delaware River

A lone eagle soars along the top of the sheer cliffs that rise above the Delaware River at Hawks Nest, New York. Two hundred and fifty feet below, in an area that nineteenth-century timber raftsmen called the "Cellar's Hole," we slow our canoe to enjoy the river's unspoiled beauty. Behind us come canoes and rafts dodging rocks and riding the two-and-a-half-foot "haystack" waves of Butler's Falls, one of the dozen or so Class I and II rapids on the Upper Delaware Scenic and Recreational River. Thanks to a combination of luck and newly acquired white-water skills, our own trip through Butler's Falls has been fast, exhilarating, and only a little wet. At that moment, the Delaware River's rich history, abundant wildlife, stunning scenery, and recreational bounty wins me as a fan forever.

From its beginning at Hancock, New York, in the foothills of the Catskill Mountains, the Delaware River flows 330 miles to the Atlantic Ocean at Cape May, New Jersey, marking the western-most border of the entire state of New Jersey and seventy-eight miles of the state line between Pennsylvania and New York. The

Delaware was discovered in 1609 by Dutch explorer Henry Hudson, who described it as "one of the finest, best and pleasantest rivers in the world," but it was too shallow for the *Half Moon*, so he headed north and found a river that suited him better.

The man for whom the Delaware was named, Thomas West, the "Twelfth Baron De-La-War," reportedly never even set eyes on the river. He was the colonial governor of the Virginia Colony, which at that time encompassed the mouth of the river. Apparently his political position earned him the honor.

The Delaware's northernmost 121 miles are part of the United States Wild and Scenic Rivers System, and are managed by the National Park Service as two distinct recreational areas: the Upper Delaware Scenic and Recreational River, a seventy-three-mile stretch of river between Hancock and Port Jervis, New York, and the Delaware Water Gap National Recreation Area, a forty-mile-long, 70,000-acre park that begins just below Port Jervis where the river crosses into New Jersey.

In these upper reaches, the Delaware's clear, free-flowing water winds through tall forests of pine, maple, and beech edged with plumes of bright purple wildflowers called loosestrife. Outcrops of shale, sandstone, and bluestone, once used for New York City sidewalks, form cliffs at several points along the shore. The banks are a feeding ground for white-tailed deer, muskrats, beavers, raccoons, opossums, and otters. You may see eagles, osprey, hawks, turkey vultures, or blue herons riding the updrafts above the hills.

There are two ways to explore the Delaware. You can drive along one of the pretty country roads that parallel the river in New York, New Jersey, and Pennsylvania, or you can rent a canoe, kayak, or raft from one of the several liveries in the Upper Delaware and Water Gap regions. You will see more from the water, but be prepared to get wet. First, the dry option.

Upper Delaware Scenic and Recreational River
New York Route 97 offers the best views of the Upper Delaware, particularly in the Hawks Nest area just north of Port Jervis, where

it takes winding S curves through a rock cut on the high river bluff. You can enjoy panoramic river views from strategically located over-looks, or you can take a more leisurely look from the Hawks Nest restaurant (914-856-9909), which combines million-dollar views with a casual atmosphere and wholesome diner-type food — all at very reasonable prices. The Hawks Nest is open seven days a week for lunch and dinner and for breakfast on weekends.

Along Route 97, you'll pass through a number of small towns with a distinctly nineteenth-century flavor — the result of what locals call "accidental preservation." Most of the structures were built between 1859 and 1915, during the prosperous days of the Delaware & Hudson (D & H) Canal. Economic hard times fol-lowed, and Delaware River Valley dwellers made do with what they had, preserving what are now historically valuable buildings.

Take time to explore the New York towns of Narrowsburg and Callicoon, and be sure to stop at the Roebling Bridge, which spans the river between Minisink Ford, New York, and Lackawax-en, Pennsylvania (about twenty-eight miles north of Port Jervis). The nearby Zane Grey Museum in Lackawaxen is also fascinating to visit.

The Roebling Bridge

The oldest existing wire suspension bridge in the United States, the Roebling Bridge was built between 1847 and 1849 by John August Roebling, who is most famous for his design of the Brooklyn Bridge. Originally created as an aqueduct for the D & H Canal and later restored as a one-lane highway crossing, the Roe-bling Bridge is still suspended on the original eight-and-a-half-inch-thick wire cables that were spun by hand at the site in the summer of 1847. The National Park Service operates a small museum and visitors center on the New York side that traces the history of the bridge and the canal, which, until 1898, carried coal barges from the Pennsylvania mines to the Hudson River near Kingston, New York. The museum is open Friday, Saturday, and Sunday, May through Labor Day. Free admission. (For more about the canal, see the D & H Canal Museum, Chapter 6.)

◆ FOR MORE INFORMATION: National Park Service, Upper Delaware Scenic and Recreational River, P.O. Box C, Narrowsburg, NY 12764; 914-252-3947 or 717-685-4871.

Zane Grey Museum

From the Roebling Bridge, it's just a short ride or walk to the Zane Grey Museum, on the Pennsylvania side of the river. Known as the father of the Western novel, Grey was a New York City dentist and avid fisherman, who gave up his practice and moved to Lackawaxen to fish and write. His first published piece was "A Day on the Delaware," which appeared in a 1902 edition of *Recreation* magazine. He wrote the most famous of his eighty-nine novels, *Riders of the Purple Sage*, while living in Lackawaxen. His former home, now a museum maintained by the National Park Service, is open for tours daily during spring and summer. Free admission.

◆ FOR MORE INFORMATION: National Park Service, Lackawaxen Access, 717- 685-4871.

Both the Zane Grey Museum and the Roebling Bridge are easy river stops for paddlers. You can beach your canoe or raft at the Lackawaxen public access area and participate in the tours, provided that you have managed to stay dry (or have a set of dry clothes to change into). No surprise: the park rangers don't want you dripping on the carefully preserved and fragile artifacts.

Delaware Water Gap National Recreational Area

The Water Gap is a geologic wonder created hundreds of millions of years ago when the river gouged through the rocks of New Jersey's Kittatinny Ridge, leaving rocky cliffs that rise 1,300 feet above a 300-foot-wide river that twists through the mountains in a tight *S* curve. The natural beauty of this area is extraordinary, with numerous waterfalls, glacial lakes, gorges, and abundant wildlife.

The Delaware Water Gap National Recreation Area, created by Congress in 1965, consists of 70,000 acres of land adjacent to the river in New Jersey and Pennsylvania. It offers more than sixty miles of hiking trails (including twenty-five miles on the Appalachian Trail), beaches, swimming areas, picnic spots, and unmatched opportunities for rock climbing, bird-watching, and fishing. There are privately operated camping areas in or nearby the Water Gap, including one accessible only by canoe, as well as state-operated camping facilities in New Jersey's Worthington State Forest, which lies within the Recreation Area.

You can enjoy the scenery if you drive along Route 209 in Pennsylvania or on New Jersey's narrow Old Mine Road, believed to be the oldest commercial highway in America, but to get the maximum impact of its awe-inspiring beauty, you should paddle a canoe through the Gap. Or if you are in shape for climbing, another astounding view is from the summit of Mount Tammany in Worthington State Forest, one of New Jersey's most challenging and popular hiking spots.

The National Park Service operates two visitors centers in the Recreation Area that have extensive literature about hiking, camping, and canoe rentals. Rangers also lead hikes and run special programs, including hawk watches in the fall. Write or call ahead for information.

◆ FOR MORE INFORMATION:

Visitors Services, Delaware Water Gap National Recreation Area, Bushkill, PA 18324; 717-588-2451.

Kittatinny Point Visitor Center, off I-80 in New Jersey; 908-496-4458.

Dingman's Falls Visitor Center PA, Route 209, Dingmans Falls, PA; 717-828-7802.

The Lower Delaware

Below the Water Gap, the Delaware is wider and less pastoral, with more commercial boat traffic and areas of industrial development along parts of the shore. There are, however, some distinct areas of interest.

The Lower Delaware's most famous visitor was, of course,

George Washington, who spent a great deal of time in the area planning his Revolutionary War offensive. River Road (NJ Route 29) from Frenchtown to Trenton will take you through a number of scenic river towns that can rightfully hang out their "George Washington Slept Here" signs.

For a quick history refresher, be sure to visit Washington Crossing State Park, which straddles the river between Titusville, New Jersey, and Washington Crossing, Pennsylvania. You will find plaques describing Washington's famous Christmas 1776 crossing of the Delaware (which is re-enacted every Christmas Day). The visitors center on the Pennsylvania side has displays of Revolutionary War artifacts and documents. The tower on Bowman's Hill (PA) alone is reason enough to visit the park, with its spectacular views of the river and Wells Falls, the Delaware's most formidable set of rapids.

Lambertville, New Jersey, and New Hope, Pennsylvania, its sister city on the western bank of the Delaware, are a hub of activity with many historic structures, restaurants, galleries, and craft and antique stores. They have the only tour boats in this section of the Delaware.

Two companies on the Pennsylvania side of the river offer scenic half-hour boat rides with music and talks highlighting the history and wildlife of the area, at prices of $5 for adults and $3 for children. Shirley and Jim Mikelionis, long-time river watchers and New Hope residents, operate the *Star of New Hope*, a thirty-seven-foot covered pontoon boat, from the dock in front of their home next to Ferry Landing Park. **Coryell's Ferry**, which traces its name and heritage to an eighteenth-century ferry operator who assisted in Washington's Delaware crossing, operates a forty-eight-seat paddlewheeler from the dock behind Gerenser's Exotic Ice Cream on South Main Street.

◆ **FOR MORE INFORMATION:**

Wells Ferry Boat Rides, 14 East Ferry Street, New Hope, PA 18938; 215-862-5965.

Coryell's Ferry, 22 South Main Street, New Hope, PA 18938; 215-862-2050.

Lambertville and New Hope are also good locations to view the historic canals that parallel the river: the Delaware & Raritan on the New Jersey side and the Delaware in Pennsylvania. The New Jersey canal is part of the state park system and is a good spot for biking or canoeing (see Chapter 6), and, in New Hope, you can actually take a ride on a mule-driven canal barge. The one-hour ride, given April through November, includes folk songs and historic tales. Adults, $6.95; children, $4.25.

◆ **FOR MORE INFORMATION**: New Hope Mule Barge Company, P.O. Box 164, New Hope, PA 18938; 215-862-2842.

Below Trenton, the Delaware becomes crowded with barges and tankers traveling from the Atlantic to Philadelphia and Wilmington, Delaware. The Camden/Philadelphia area has some recreational activity, with the New Jersey State Aquarium in Camden (see Chapter 7) and boat rides from Philadelphia's restored Penn's Landing waterfront. As it flows closer to the Atlantic, the Delaware becomes a broad bay, more seacoast than river.

Canoeing and Rafting

The Delaware River is a paddler's delight, offering both long stretches of quiet water that run through areas of spectacular scenery and enough rapids and rifts to trigger an occasional adrenaline rush and offer thrills without a lot of danger. The largest rapids in Delaware are Class II on the International Scale of River Difficulty, meaning they have waves of up to three feet with generally clear channels, but they require some maneuvering around rocky areas. (Class VI is the most difficult, and Class III is generally the highest possible for an open canoe.)

Still, if you are new to paddling, the National Park Service advises that you select a flat-water section on which to learn basic canoe skills or enjoy the white water from a raft or tube, which are more forgiving. The forty-mile stretch of river within the Delaware

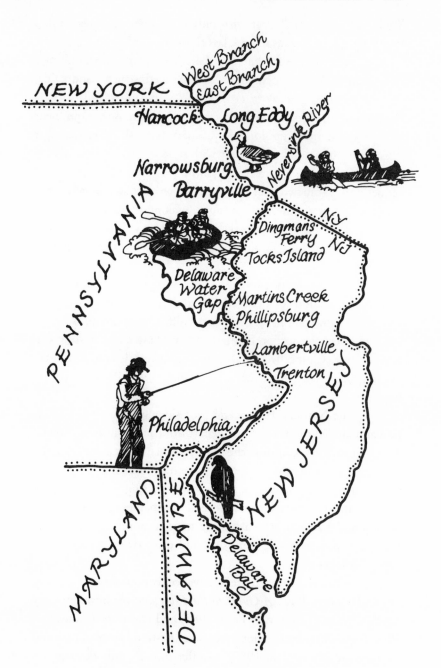

Water Gap is generally flat with only occasional unclassed riffles; the Upper Delaware has seven Class II rapids.

"The difference between lake and river canoeing," says Ranger Kitty Womer, a National Park Service instructor and guide, "is the difference between cross-country and downhill skiing." Except in unusual conditions, the Upper Delaware is the equivalent of an easy intermediate slope. If you have basic skills, you can get through it, though not necessarily with style.

This natural water playground has approximately 8,000 canoes and a somewhat smaller number of rafts and kayaks available for rent at a variety of locations, making it the most popular canoeing location in New York and New Jersey. But unlike commercial water parks, it is never so crowded that you can't enjoy its wild beauty.

Nearly twenty companies rent boats and provide return road transportation for between $25 and $30 per person per day. Often the same company has several different operating sites, so you can select the section of the river that best matches your skill and interest. Canoe liveries also provide life jackets and a safety briefing before you begin what is usually a ten-mile, four-to-five-hour trip.

The National Park Service occasionally offers free instruction and guided canoe trips that depart from access areas near rental sites. Kittatinny Canoes, the largest and oldest livery on the Delaware, has a number of special programs, including basic canoe and white-water instruction, canoe trips for singles, and summer wildlife and fall foliage tours. Several companies, including Kittatinny and Lander's, which has the most locations on the Upper Delaware, have riverside campsites and offer two-day camp-and-canoe packages.

If you want to prepare in advance, two books — *Canoeing on the Delaware River. A Guide to the River and the Shore* by Gary Letcher (Rutgers University Press, 1985) and *Down the Delaware, A River Users' Guide* by Charlotte McCabe (Eastern National Park and Monument Association, 1987) — offer mile-by-mile descriptions of every rock and rapid from Hancock to Trenton, as well as fascinating accounts of the area's geology, history, and local lore.

◆ **FOR MORE INFORMATION:** The National Park Service has a twenty-four-hour river hot line (914-252-7100) that reports Upper Delaware River conditions, including river depth and speed, and alerts boaters when unusual river conditions require advanced boating skill. The following are all licensed commercial canoe liveries operating in or near the Upper Delaware and/or Delaware Water Gap areas.

Adventure Sports Canoe and Raft Trips, Inc., Route 209, Box 175, Marshalls Creek, PA 18335; 800-487-2628.

Cedar Rapids Canoe and Kayak, Route 97, Box 219, Barryville, NY 12719; 914-557-6158.

Chamberlain's Canoes, Inc., Minisink Acres, Minisink Hills, PA 18341; 800-422-6631.

Delaware River Rafting and Canoeing, Route 46, Box 142, Delaware, NJ 07833; 800-543-0271.

Indian Head Canoes and Rafts (three locations), Route 97, Pond Eddy, NY; 800-874-2628.

Kittatinny Canoes (six locations), Route 739, Dingman's Ferry, PA 18328; 800-FLOAT-KC (356-2852).

Lander's Delaware River Trips (nine locations), Route 97, Narrowsburg, NY 12764; 800-252-3925.

Long Eddy Canoe Rental, P.O. Box 5, Long Eddy, NY 12760; 914-887-4178.

Pack Shack Adventures, Inc., Box 127, 88 Broad Street, Delaware Water Gap, PA 18327; 800-424-0955.

Point Pleasant Canoes and Tubes, Box 6, Point Pleasant, PA; 215-297-8823.

Shawnee Canoe Trips, River Road, Shawnee-on-Delaware, PA 18358; 800-SHAWNEE, ext. 1120.

Silver Canoe Rentals, 37 South Maple Avenue, Port Jervis, NY 12771; 914-856-7055.

T & W Canoes, Route 46, Box 1796, RD 1, Columbia, NJ 07832; 908-475-4608.

Three River Canoe Corp. (three locations), Box 7, Pond Eddy, NY; 914-557-6078.

Tri-State Canoes, Box 400, Shay Lane, Matamoras, PA; 800-56-CANOE (562-2663).

Two River Junction, HC Box 1A, Scenic Drive, Lackawaxen, PA 18435; 717-685-2010.

White Water Willie's, 17 West Main Street, Port Jervis, NY 12771; 800-233-RAFT (233-7238).

Wild and Scenic River Tours, 166 Route 97, Barryville, NY 12719; 800-836-0366.

Tubing

Skinners Falls, named for Daniel Skinner, who launched the Delaware River's first timber-rafting business in 1764, are the largest and most challenging rapids on the Upper Delaware. Featured on the *Today Show* as one of the top swimming holes in America, Skinners Falls is nature's own water park with beautiful scenery and rapids that race down four small rock ledges, making an exciting spot for tubing and rafting and the upper river's biggest challenge for canoeists.

◆ **FOR MORE INFORMATION:** Two local companies rent tubes at the Skinners Falls Public Access area: Lou's Tubes, P.O. Box 11, Milanville, PA 18443, 914-252-3593; and Lander's River Trips, Route 97, Narrowsburg, NY, 800-252-3925.

Fishing

The Delaware is a popular fishing stream, famous for brown and rainbow trout, smallmouth bass, walleye, and shad, which swim upstream by the tens of thousands during the spring spawning season, their dorsal fins breaking the surface of the water in a wondrous dance pattern. During August and September, eels swim downriver toward the ocean, with thousands ending their migration, and their lives, in the elaborate eel weirs that look like ski jumps in the middle of the river. The weirs, made up of two stone walls that form a downstream *V* with a wooden trap in the center, are an example of a fishing tradition that dates back to the Lenni Lanape Indians, who lived along the river until the late eighteenth century. They are also an obstacle to be avoided by canoeists and rafters. Depending on the section of the river you choose for fishing, you will need a license from New York, New Jersey, or Pennsylvania.

River Resources

The National Park Service runs a tremendous variety of programs about the heritage and natural resources of the Delaware. These include canoe lessons, hikes, nature walks and talks, walking tours of Revolutionary War sites, and programs about local Native American culture and life on the Delaware & Hudson Canal. Books, brochures, river safety films, and vacation planning assistance are available at information centers.

◆ **FOR MORE INFORMATION:**

National Park Service, Upper Delaware Scenic and Recreational River, Narrowsburg Information Center, Main Street, Narrowsburg, NY 12764; 914- 252-2947.

Delaware Water Gap National Recreation Area, Visitors Services, Delaware Water Gap National Recreation Area, Bushkill, PA 18324; 717-588-2451.

Kittatinny Point Visitor Center; 908-496-4458.

Dingman's Falls Visitor Center; 717-828-7802.

The Upper Delaware Council, a regional planning agency, publishes an excellent guide to the region and a quarterly newsletter of river news and events. Upper Delaware Council, 211 Bridge Street, P.O. Box 217, Narrowsburg, NY 12764; 914-252-3022.

The Delaware Riverkeeper Project, an affiliate of the American Littoral Society that works to "preserve, protect, and enhance the Delaware River, its habitats, and its wildlife," has an active group of volunteers who monitor river conditions and sponsor special river events. Delaware Riverkeeper, P.O. Box 753, Lambertville, NJ 08530; 609-397-4410.

◆ 6 ◆
Locks and Legends: New York and New Jersey Canals

New York State Canal Recreationway

By the time I finished fourth grade, I could spout off all the essential facts about the Erie Canal: "Clinton's Ditch," as the first great U.S. canal was called, was an engineering marvel that cut a watery path for 363 miles across New York State, carrying boats uphill from the Hudson River to Lake Erie. Its opening in 1825 made it possible to travel by boat from New York City to the Mississippi River, a linkage that spurred westward trade and migration and made New York City the greatest port in the United States. My history book called it the "Eighth Wonder of the World."

But it was not until last year, when I cruised on the canal from western New York State to Troy, my former hometown, that I began to appreciate the incredible beauty and remarkable technology of this man-made waterway. My eyes actually teared when we descended the "Waterford Flight," a stairlike quintuplet of locks that lifts or lowers boats a distance of 169 feet in a little more than a mile. These locks, regarded as the greatest set of high-lift locks in the world, are less than two miles from the grammar school where I'd memorized those canal facts. How come I'd never seen them before?

Until fairly recently, the recreational potential of New York's canal system was one of the state's best-kept secrets. Through World War II, the canals were crowded with heavy freight barges, first pulled by mules, later by powerful tugs. But after the war, highways and the opening of the St. Lawrence Seaway in 1959 made canal transport obsolete. For a time, the canals were almost forgotten, and many people feared New York State would abandon them. But gradually, boaters started using them for recreation.

In 1992, New York State officials designated the New York State Canal System as a "recreationway." Their goal since has been to promote the romance of canal travel and to make the system user-friendly for those of us interested in exploring a 524-mile scenic waterway and living-history trail.

The canal's four sections — Champlain, Cayuga-Seneca, Oswego, and Erie — link the Hudson River, Lake Champlain, the Finger Lakes, Lake Ontario, and Lake Erie, and offer scores of wonderful vacation opportunities, some of which can be enjoyed in as little as an afternoon. Since New York's major highways parallel the canals, most attractions are easily accessible by car.

Parks are adjacent to several locks, and canal-side bike and hiking trails follow many of the old towpaths, where mules like "Sal" once did their "fifteen miles on the Erie Canal." Marinas, restaurants, and picnic areas border the canals, and a number of different boating options, from commercial cruises to drive-yourself rental boats, are available. In 1994, about 150,000 boats, including privately operated pleasure boats, tour boats, and a small number of tugs and barges, locked through the system. Several towns celebrate their canal heritage with festivals between May and October.

◆ **FOR MORE INFORMATION:** The New York State Canal Corporation publishes a guide to events and attractions throughout the system and maintains a telephone hot line listing special events. NYS Canal Corp., P.O. Box 189, Albany, NY 12201; 800-4-CANAL-4 (800-422-6254).

Locking Through

New York's canals have been expanded, rerouted, and modernized twice since Governor DeWitt Clinton defied many nineteenth-century doubters and built the Erie. But its existing replacement, the New York State Barge Canal, is itself an old-timer. Built between 1905 and 1918, it combines twisting "canalized" rivers and arrow-straight man-made cuts with a system of locks, dams, and lift bridges, most of which survive today in their original

NEW YORK STATE CANALS

form. Indeed, part of the charm of the canal is the antiquity of the equipment that operates it.

The locks themselves are wonders of simplicity. Once you accept two basic physical principles — water flows downhill, and it always seeks its own level — it is easy to understand how they work. It's all a matter of gravity, valves, and gates. Think of the lock as a giant bathtub (300 feet long and 43.5 feet wide throughout the New York State system) with stoppers at either end. When a boat enters a lock from downstream, it's at the bottom of a fairly empty tub. The lock tender closes the downstream gate and valve, opens the upstream valve, and water pours into the opening from above, filling a tunnel beside the canal wall. Since the valve at the bottom is closed, the water then flows out openings in the side of the tunnel, filling the lock. When the water levels in the lock and the upstream waterway are equal, the flow stops on its own. To empty the lock, the process is reversed.

The first time you enter a lock chamber, it is exciting — perhaps even a little intimidating if you are driving your own boat — to watch the gates close behind you and hear valves opening and water gurgling. But everything happens slowly (the whole process takes about fifteen minutes) and you rise (or descend) smoothly, gradually — just like a toy boat in a bathtub — as the water level changes in the lock. Then the gate opens and you power out ten, twenty, or more feet above (or below) where you entered the lock. By the third lock, it's routine, but still impressive. Be sure to ask a lock tender to show you how it all works. Many are second- or third-generation canalers who take special pride in sharing their heritage and showing off their beautifully maintained eighty-year-old canal works.

Canal Boats

Whether you are taking a two-hour tour or piloting your own craft for a week's cruise, it's refreshing to leave the hurry-up world behind and travel in the slow lane (maximum speed 10 mph!) where you can enjoy the canal's diverse landscape: lush farms, old factories, blue herons nesting near the Montezuma

Wildlife Refuge in central New York, the Appalachian Mountains rising above the Champlain Canal, pretty canal towns, and even substantial cities that flourished in the wake of canal development. You see communities where time has taken its toll and others enjoying a waterfront rebirth.

Boating opportunities are plentiful and include something to suit almost every calendar and pocketbook. Most boats operate from May to October. Unless otherwise indicated, prices listed are actual 1994 rates. Call ahead for reservations and updated price information.

DRIVE-YOURSELF RENTAL BOATS

Mid-Lakes Navigation Company, Ltd., brought the magic of European-style canal cruising to New York with the 1987 introduction of what the company calls "Lockmaster" Hireboats. Designed to resemble the family-sized narrow boats that ply the canals of France and England, these sturdy, steel-hulled vessels have flat roofs, tiller steering, and large well-equipped cabins with galleys, showers, heads, and, depending on the size of the particular boat, berths for between four and eight people. With diesel engines and electric bow-thrusters to aid in docking, Lockmasters are easy to operate after a short hands-on orientation — even for first-time boaters. Living aboard your own canalboat, you set the pace, choose the route, and enjoy the challenge and satisfaction of being the captain.

Mid-Lakes, which builds all Lockmasters, has six for charter (thirty-three to forty-four feet long) on the western part of the Erie Canal between May and October. Prices depend on boat size and season, ranging from $1,200 to $2,000 per week (for everything but food).

◆ **FOR MORE INFORMATION:** Mid-Lakes Navigation Co., Ltd., 11 Jordan Street, P.O. Box 61, Skaneateles, NY 13152; 800-545-4318.

Collar City Charters, located in Troy near the first lock of the canal system, operates a similar charter program using four forty-one-foot Lockmasters, which are available for weekly self-captained cruises through the eastern part of the Erie Canal, the Champlain Canal, or the Hudson River. Weekly prices for 1995 are $1,500 (May and October) and $1,700 (June through September).

◆ **FOR MORE INFORMATION:** Collar City Charters, 427 River Street, Troy, NY 12180; 518-272-5341.

OVERNIGHT CRUISES

Emita II, the flagship of Mid-Lakes Navigation's canal fleet, makes two- and three-day cruises through New York's canal system. What you lose in independence by choosing the *Emita II* over a drive-yourself charter you get back in warmth and rich information. Capt. Dan Wiles, the son of the Mid-Lakes founder, grew up on the canal and shares his father's love, knowledge, and strong opinions about canal traditions, which he willingly imparts throughout every cruise. The atmosphere is wonderfully homey, and the cruise is particularly popular with older people who enjoy traveling at a relaxed pace. Many are repeat customers.

A refitted 1950s vintage, sixty-five-foot Casco Bay (Maine) ferry, *Emita II* carries forty-five passengers and has an open top deck and a comfortable enclosed, wood-paneled main cabin with a library, bar, and dining room. Passengers eat meals aboard and travel by bus to nearby motels to spend the night.

Three-day itineraries include a western Erie cruise between Syracuse and Buffalo, a central New York cruise between Syracuse and Albany, and a round-trip cruise from Troy to Whitehall on the Champlain Canal. Two-day trips travel the Oswego or Cayuga-Seneca Canals from Syracuse. All trips offer lock tours and shore visits to historic sites, but the real destination is the canal itself. Prices range from $222 to $489, including all meals and accommodations. Three-day canal trips between Buffalo, Syracuse, and Albany are one-way, with return bus transportation provided.

◆ **FOR MORE INFORMATION:** Mid-Lakes Navigation Co., Ltd., 11 Jordan Street, P.O. Box 61, Skaneateles, NY 13152; 800-545-4318.

The *Niagara Prince*, the newest of the small cruise ships operated by the **American/Canadian/Caribbean Line**, was designed with the Erie Canal in mind. Launched in November 1994, this 175-foot, eighty-four-passenger vessel has wrap-around windows and a retractable wheelhouse that allows it to pass beneath the Erie's lowest bridge, just sixteen feet, two inches. *Niagara Prince* begins twelve-day cruises in summer 1995, traveling from Rhode Island to the Hudson River via Long Island Sound, then to Vermont and back through the Champlain Canal, and finally west to Buffalo on the Erie, with stops along the way. (Somehow it's nice to know that the Champlain Canal makes it possible to cruise from the ocean to the northern borders of New England's only noncoastal state.) The Niagara's sister ships, *Caribbean Prince* and *Mayan Prince*, also do Erie Canal cruises. All accommodations and meals are onboard in an atmosphere that is comfort-filled but casual. No neckties, please! Prices: $1,300 to $2,950, depending on schedule and cabin choice.

◆ **FOR MORE INFORMATION:** American/Canadian/Caribbean Lines, Inc., P.O. Box 368, Warren, RI 02885; 800-556-7450 or 401-247-0995.

Grace, a luxury troller, takes up to six passengers on three-day canal vacations on the Erie or Champlain Canal. Guests stay in country inns and visit historic sites along the way. Prices start at $399 and include meals and accommodations.

◆ **FOR MORE INFORMATION:** Premier Charter, P.O. Box 161, Feura Bush, NY 12067; 518-768-2154.

SIGHTSEEING AND DINING CRUISES

Mid-Lakes Navigation's day boat, the *City of Syracuse*, sails from its namesake city with lunch, dinner, and sightseeing cruises on the Erie Canal and Onondaga Lake, some with live entertainment. Most trips make two passes through Lock 24 in Baldwinsville. Tickets: $7.50 to $32.00; less for children and family groups.

◆ **FOR MORE INFORMATION:** Mid-Lakes Navigation Co., Ltd., 11 Jordan Street, P.O. Box 61, Skaneateles, NY 13152; 800-545-4318.

Captain Dave Conroy, owner/operator of the tour boat *Liberty,* is a self-proclaimed "river rat" who has spent his whole life working on the canal, first as a lock operator, later as a tugboat captain. Now retired, he runs canal cruises from the town of Lyons (between Syracuse and Rochester) on *Liberty,* a restored forty-nine-passenger former navy launch. Highlights include a lock visit and Conroy's well-informed narration. Group tours and "walk-up" sightseeing trips are offered. Call for schedule and prices.

◆ **FOR MORE INFORMATION:** Liberty Cruises, 37 Layton Street, Lyons, NY 14489; 315-946-4108.

Colonial Belle, a 220-passenger paddle-wheeler, is the largest tour boat regularly operating on the Erie Canal. Sailing out of Fairport (just east of Rochester), it offers narrated tours through a section of the canal that retains much of its nineteenth-century flavor. Lunch, dinner, and special lock cruises are scheduled Tuesday through Sunday. Prices: $10 and up.

◆ **FOR MORE INFORMATION:** *Colonial Belle*, 4 Burling Gap, Fairport, NY 14460; 716-377-4600.

Named for a daredevil waterfall jumper from western New York, the *Sam Patch* is a traditionally styled forty-nine-passenger canal packet boat that offers canal and river trips from downtown Rochester. A not-for-profit organization, the Corn Hill Waterfront and Navigation Foundation, runs both sightseeing and dinner cruises and contributes profits to a dedicated fund for the enhancement of Rochester's Corn Hill Riverfront. Prices: $10 (sightseeing) to $37.50 (dinner); seniors and children less.

◆ **FOR MORE INFORMATION:** Corn Hill Waterfront and Navigation Foundation, 250 Exchange Boulevard, Rochester, NY 14608; 716-262-5661.

Miss Apple Grove, the only mule-drawn packet boat left on the Erie, runs two-hour trips through the historic town of Medina, a popular stop for early canalers, since it was about a day by boat from both Buffalo and Rochester. Count on being entertained by the captain's stories, some banjo playing, and the antics of the mule drivers on the towpath. Light refreshments are available, and the Apple Grove Inn, which operates the boat, serves a buffet lunch after the tour. Tickets: $23 (boat and buffet); $10 (boat ride only).

◆ **FOR MORE INFORMATION:** *Miss Apple Grove*, 11104 West Center Street Ext., Medina, NY 14103; 716-798-2323.

During the two-hour cruise that **Lockport Locks and Canal Tours** describes as "historic but fun," you'll be lifted fifty feet through two locks and travel under two early-twentieth-century lift bridges, as well as an "upside down" railroad bridge. You will also pass by five original locks from the 1825 canal and the only drydock left in the western Erie. The company operates two tour boats, *Lockview III* and *Lockview IV*. Snacks and liquor bar onboard. 1995 prices: $10 for adults; $7 for kids. Group rates available.

◆ **FOR MORE INFORMATION:** Lockport Locks and Canal Tours, 304 Irving Drive, Tonawanda, NY 14150; 716-693-3260.

Three Hudson River cruise operators from the Albany/Troy area — Capt. J. P. Cruise Lines, Dutch Apple Cruises, Inc., and Pegasus Riverboat Company — run occasional sightseeing trips through the Troy Lock. See Chapter 4.

Historic Attractions

THE *URGER*

The tugboat *Urger* is a moving living-history exhibit that belongs in a class by itself. Built in 1901 as a Great Lakes fishing tug, the *Urger* has been a workhorse on New York state's canals since 1922. After hauling machinery, dredges, and scows for nearly seven decades, the *Urger* became an educational vessel in 1991. With Capt. Steve Wunder and a crew of long-time canalers and buffs, the Urger now travels through the canal system keeping towboat traditions alive and telling the story of old-time canaling to school groups and festival visitors. Visitors can tour the boat at dockside (no rides), turn its large brass wheel, and communicate with the engine room through an old-fashioned bell system. The *Urger* also carries a model lock, and by 1995 hopes to have a model steam engine aboard.

◆ **FOR MORE INFORMATION:** *Urger,* c/o New York State Canal Corporation, P.O. Box 189, Albany, NY 12210; 800-4-CANAL-4.

ERIE CANAL VILLAGE

Located in Rome, New York, on the site where workers began digging the Erie Canal on July 4, 1817, the Erie Canal

Tugboat Urger, *a workhorse on the New York State Canal System since 1922*

Village is a re-created canal town, with historic buildings (moved from nearby locations), a living-history exhibit, and a museum depicting canal history. The highlight of any visit is a ride in an 1840s-style horse-drawn passenger boat along a refurbished section of the old Erie, where a narrator tells stories about the canal and leads songs like "Low Bridge, Everybody Down."

◆ FOR MORE INFORMATION: Erie Canal Village, 5789 New London Road, Rome, NY 13440; 315-337-3999. Located about eighty miles northwest of Albany, near exits 32 and 33 of the NYS Thruway. Open daily May through September. Admission is charged. Schedule and prices subject to change.

CANASTOTA CANAL TOWN MUSEUM

Canastota, a small town located near Oneida Lake, enjoyed a great boom during the heyday of the Erie Canal. Its small museum has artifacts and pictures of the old canal that would be of particular interest to history buffs.

◆ FOR MORE INFORMATION: Canastota Canal Town Museum, 122 Canal Street, P.O. Box 51, Canastota, NY 13032; 315-697-3451. Call for hours.

ERIE CANAL MUSEUM

The Erie Canal Museum in Syracuse sees its mission as "telling the great adventure story of the canal's history." Housed in the landmarked Weighlock Building, the only surviving Erie Canal boat weighing station, the museum has a theater presentation, photographs, artifacts, and hands-on exhibits that evoke busy canal days. Visitors can climb aboard and explore the crew quarters, cargo hold, and passenger compartment of the *Frank Buchanan Thomson*, a sixty-five-foot, full-size replica of a nineteenth-century canalboat. Operated by a not-for-profit organization, the museum sponsors an active program of community events and maintains a research library that is open to the public by appointment.

◆ FOR MORE INFORMATION: Erie Canal Museum, 318 Erie Boulevard East, Syracuse, NY 13202; 315-471-0593. Open year-round, seven days a week. Free admission.

Other New York and New Jersey Canals

The success of the Erie Canal touched off a great flurry of canal building, and by 1840, the combined length of the canals in the United States exceeded 4,000 miles. Among these were three New York and New Jersey canals that played a vital role in commercial transport from the 1830s to the early 1900s. Two — the Delaware & Hudson and the Morris — are kept alive by museums; the third, New Jersey's Delaware & Raritan, survives as a popular canoeing spot within a state park.

DELAWARE & HUDSON CANAL

The D & H Canal Museum in High Falls, New York, tells the story of the 108-mile canal between Pennsylvania and Rondout Creek on the Hudson River. Built by hand between 1825 and 1828, the canal was, for sixty years, a vital link in the transport of coal from the mines of Pennsylvania to New York City. The museum shows maps, photos, and artifacts of the canal and the boomtowns along its route. There is also a walking tour of some surviving nineteenth-century locks. The Roebling Bridge over the Delaware River (see Chapter 5) was once a D & H Canal aqueduct. Open May through October. Call for schedule. Nominal admission charge.

◆ **FOR MORE INFORMATION:** Canal Museum of the D & H Canal Historical Society, P.O. Box 23, High Falls, NY 12440; 914-687-9311.

MORRIS CANAL

The 102-mile Morris Canal, built between 1824 and 1831, was the "highest climbing" of all the early canals in the United States. It ran from Phillipsburg on the Delaware River to Newark Bay, climbing 760 feet to its summit level at Lake Hopatcong in central New Jersey, then dropping 914 feet to the bay, using a technologically innovative system of inclined planes, water turbines, and locks. The Morris was a thriving cargo route for coal, iron ore, grain, and lumber throughout the nineteenth century. Eventually, it was eclipsed by the railroads and abandoned in 1924. Although much of the canal has been destroyed (Newark's subway runs in the old canal bed), remains of inclined planes and water turbines survive at various locations along the old canal route; some are being restored by local groups.

At Waterloo Village, a reconstructed Morris Canal town located about an hour west of New York City on Route 80, it is possible to see an inclined plane, which is slated for restoration, a lift lock, and a mule bridge. The Canal Society of New Jersey operates an excellent Canal Museum at Waterloo, which displays a working model of an inclined plane as well as photographs and artifacts. On weekends, members of the Canal Society of New Jersey act as guides and are a wonderful source of colorful information about New Jersey's canals. Waterloo Village also has restored period homes, costumed guides, and artisans, and it sponsors a highly regarded arts festival from May to October, which features concerts and performances by internationally acclaimed artists of all kinds. Admission to the village: $8 adults; children and seniors less. Additional charge for concerts.

◆ FOR MORE INFORMATION:

Waterloo Village, Waterloo Road, Stanhope, NJ 07874; 201-347-0900.

Canal Society of New Jersey, P.O. Box 737, Morristown, NJ 07963; 908-722-9556.

DELAWARE & RARITAN CANAL

The Delaware & Raritan Canal, competed in 1834, was the main inland water link between Philadelphia and New York, and for a time its traffic occasionally exceeded that of the Erie Canal. Like other industrial canals, its heyday ended in the early 1900s, but the D & R survives today as a sixty-four-mile New Jersey State Park, with hiking, horse, and bike trails along the old towpath and canoe access areas and rental places. The site of the original outlet locks can still be seen along the Raritan River in New Brunswick.

◆ **FOR MORE INFORMATION:**

Delaware & Raritan Canal State Park, 643 Canal Road, Somerset, NJ 08873; 908-873-3050.

Canoe rentals: Griggstown Canoes, Griggstown, NJ; 908-359-5970.

Black Bottom Canoes, Princeton, NJ; 609-452-2403.

◆ 7 ◆
Natural Treasures:
Whale Watches, Aquariums,
Beach Walks,
and Nature Preserves

Reed grass six feet tall borders a winding path that leads through marshland toward an open bay. A muskrat darts by, and a snowy egret stands at the marsh's edge. Near the shore, a half dozen geese look for food. The path curves, and in the distance, the twin towers of the World Trade Center and the Lower Manhattan skyline appear on the horizon, a startling reminder that the peaceful wildlife refuge we are exploring is just a subway ride away from the concrete city we've left behind.

In New York and New Jersey, states best known for their densely populated urban centers, nature preserves like the Gateway National Recreation Area's Jamaica Bay Wildlife Refuge (described above) often evoke surprise. But, in fact, these two states are filled with forests, wetlands, beaches, and waterways that teem with wildlife. Strategically located on the Atlantic Flyway, they have some of the world's best bird-watching spots. Tidal estuaries in

Delaware Bay, the Hudson River, and coastal areas in both states are important spawning areas for Atlantic Coast fish, and, just a few miles from shore, whales and dolphins swim in ocean waters.

Although development has sadly encroached on some natural areas, damaging habitats and endangering species, many places have been preserved, and, as a result of increasing environmental awareness, new nature refuges and programs are continually being established. This chapter describes whale and dolphin watching cruises, as well as some of the aquariums, wildlife areas, nature programs, and bird observatories that celebrate and teach about New York's and New Jersey's wonderful natural treasures.

Whale Watch and Nature Cruises

The *Viking Starship*, a large whale watching vessel operated by the **Okeanos Ocean Research Foundation, Inc.**, passes Montauk Lighthouse and heads seaward. The 200 or so people onboard scan the horizon in eager anticipation as the vessel makes its way toward an area where finback whales were seen the day before. Prospects are good. "But," the naturalist warns, "there are never any guarantees with wildlife."

People have been pursuing whales from Northeast ports for several centuries. First, Long Island's Montaukett Indians captured them, taking blubber for food and tail flukes for religious sacrifices; later, nineteenth-century whaling captains chased whales around the world in search of fortunes made from sperm oil. Now modern whalers come, armed with cameras instead of harpoons, seeking education and entertainment.

Okeanos, a nonprofit education and research organization founded in 1980, operates the only whale watch cruises in New York State. In New Jersey, several Cape May County boat operators combine whale and dolphin watches with sightseeing excursions.

New York

Whale watches further Okeanos's educational mission by introducing people to the extraordinary majesty of these creatures

— the largest mammals that ever lived — and teaching about the importance of protection for these endangered species.

Based on their own research data and on reports from a cooperative network of local fishermen, Okeanos scientists generally know the best areas to look for whales. "But the technology for sighting and spotting whales is no different than it was hundreds of years ago," says Okeanos research director Samuel Sadove. "We just look for the blow in the distance."

"Two o'clock," the naturalist says, directing people aboard the *Viking Starship* to look off to the right, and there, after nearly ninety minutes at sea, they see a receding spume of water and a mammoth dark-colored animal breaking the surface of the water, not more than 200 yards away. The boat throttles back and advances slowly, as passengers exhale a collective sigh of relief and head to the rail for a better look.

The next two hours are a series of "ooohs" and "ahs" as three finback whales — sixty to seventy feet long and over 100,000 pounds each — feed, dive, and play in the vicinity of the boat. Okeanos scientists study the whales, taking photos, timing dives, monitoring respiration rates, and explaining whale behavior as best they can. Finbacks rarely breach (leap out of the ocean) but they do roll and bring their tail flukes partially out of the water, rub up against one another (rowdy, pre-mating behavior), dive, and come close enough to the boat that passengers can feel the spray from their blow.

Finback whales, believed to reside in the waters off Long Island, are the species most often seen on the cruises that depart from Montauk. But the area also attracts migrating humpbacks (generally more playful and inclined to breaching), minke whales (up to thirty feet), and relatively rare sperm whales.

What you will see on a whale watch cruise is impossible to predict. Okeanos claims an above 90 percent success rate during July and August. During May, June, and September, when whales are migrating, there is a greater variety of species, but fewer whales overall. The success rate then is closer to 70 percent. Dolphins, seabirds, and other marine life add interest during many cruises.

In Greek mythology, Okeanos is the father of all life in the sea; in New York, Okeanos is the only state and federally licensed marine mammal stranding and rescue program. The organization generally assists in about 150 rescues a year. In addition, Okeanos conducts extensive marine mammal research, runs seal watch cruises during winter and early spring, leads nature walks, and sponsors other marine education programs. It operates a visitors center in Hampton Bays, and is currently developing a major aquarium, scheduled to open in Riverhead, Long Island, in 1997. Whale watches, which leave from the Viking Dock in Montauk, last four to six hours and operate from May 15 through September, weather permitting. Price: $28 adult; $15 children.

◆ **FOR MORE INFORMATION:** Okeanos Ocean Research Foundation, Inc., P.O. Box 776, Hampton Bays, NY 11946; 516-728-4522.

New Jersey

The waters off Cape May, where the Atlantic Ocean meets Delaware Bay, have become a summer home and major calving area for American bottlenose dolphins. Up to 4,000 dolphins have

reportedly been seen in a single day. These graceful gray marine mammals often swim in family groups, three-foot-long babies seemingly playing follow-the-leader with their ten-foot mothers. Dolphins are extremely active and social, and their antics provide almost constant entertainment. Most boat operators have a narrator or an onboard naturalist who interprets behavior and tells interesting dolphin stories. Cruises are relatively short (about two hours), which makes them ideal for children.

Whale watching off the New Jersey coast is a hit-or-miss affair. Whales travel through these waters during spring and fall on their way north or south, but they tend not to stay a long time. Although many cruises are called "whale and dolphin watches," the likelihood of seeing whales in summer is only about 10 percent, according to the Marine Mammal Stranding Center in Brigantine, New Jersey. The dolphin success rate is above 90 percent.

◆ FOR MORE INFORMATION: The following companies offer marine mammal sightseeing cruises or nature excursions. Since schedules, prices, destinations, and emphases vary, it is best to call in advance for trip descriptions.

Big Flamingo, Sinn's Dock, 6006 Park Boulevard, Wildwood Crest, NJ; 609-522-3934.

Cape May Whale Watcher, Second Avenue and Wilson Drive, Cape May, NJ 08240; 609-884-5445.

Cape May Whale Watch and Research Center, 1286 Wilson Drive, Cape May, NJ 08240; 609-898-0055

Captain Schumann's Big Blue Sightseer, 4500 Park Boulevard, Wildwood, NJ 08260; 609-522-2919.

Jersey Cape Nature Excursions, Miss Chris Marina, Third Avenue and Wilson Drive, Cape May, NJ 08294.

North Star, Palen Avenue, Ocean City, NJ 08226; 609-399-7588.

Ocean Discovery Center, 1121 Route 109, Cape May, NJ 08260; 609-898-0999.

Princess Cruises, City Marina, 42nd Street and the Bay, Sea Isle City, NJ; 609-263-1633.

The **Marine Mammal Stranding Center**, located just north of Atlantic City in Brigantine, is, like Okeanos, a nonprofit organization licensed to rescue and rehabilitate stranded whales, dolphins, and other endangered marine species. Although it does not run regular whale or dolphin watch cruises, the center sometimes sponsors special naturalist-led excursions or knows of worthwhile nature cruises run by other groups. Staff members may also be able to help you evaluate some of the available commercial cruises. The Stranding Center operates a small museum in the town of Brigantine. Open weekends, year-round; daily in summer. Free admission.

◆ **FOR MORE INFORMATION:** Marine Mammal Stranding Center, 3625 Brigantine Boulevard, Brigantine, NJ 08203; 609-266-0538.

Aquariums

Aquarium for Wildlife Conservation

Located at Coney Island Beach in Brooklyn, New York, the Aquarium for Wildlife Conservation, known locally as the New York Aquarium, is a place where whales watch people. Six beluga whales, including two young aquarium-born belugas, swim right up to the picture window in their 400,000-gallon seawater tank, and seemingly look visitors right in the eye.

The aquarium, which was founded in 1896, also has sharks, sea otters, walruses, penguins, seals, and thousands of fish swimming in over a hundred tanks. Discovery Cove, a hands-on exhibit that emphasizes the relationship between people and the sea, is both unusual and effective. Open 365 days a year. Admission: $6.75 adults; $2 seniors and children under twelve.

◆ **FOR MORE INFORMATION:** Aquarium for Wildlife Conservation, West 8th Street and Surf Avenue, Brooklyn, NY 11224; 718-265-FISH.

New Jersey State Aquarium

Located in downtown Camden overlooking the Delaware River directly across from the City of Philadelphia, the $52 million New Jersey State Aquarium opened in 1992, with a 760,000-gallon "open ocean" tank — the second largest in the world — and two

"touch tanks," which offer opportunities to stroke sharks and sea stars. The aquarium also has an outdoor seal pool, where gray seals and harbor seals swim, and a number of special exhibits. The emphasis is on wildlife native to the waters and wetlands of New Jersey and the North Atlantic, with displays about barrier beaches, the New Jersey Pine Barrens, the Delaware River, and Delaware Bay. Aquatic activities for children and workshops for adults are also offered. Open year-round. Admission: $9 adults; $6 children ages two through eleven.

◆ **FOR MORE INFORMATION:** Thomas H. Kean New Jersey State Aquarium at Camden, 1 Riverside Drive, Camden, NJ 08103; 609-365-3300.

Cold Spring Harbor Fish Hatchery and Aquarium

After ninety-nine years in business as a trout hatchery, this Long Island facility became a nonprofit educational hatchery and aquarium in 1982. Visitors can see both newly hatched and developing trout, raised for stocking private ponds, and, on fall weekends, watch egg-stripping demonstrations. Other displays include an aquarium with freshwater fish, amphibians, and aquatic reptiles, all native to New York waters. Children especially will enjoy the turtle collection, with ten species of New York State turtles, including Junior, a seventy-two-pound common snapping turtle, estimated to be between eighty and one hundred years old. The hatchery also runs a number of environmental education programs for school groups. Open year-round. Small admission charge.

◆ **FOR MORE INFORMATION:** Cold Spring Harbor Fish Hatchery and Aquarium, P.O. Box 535, Cold Spring Harbor, NY 11724; 516-692-6768.

The River Project

Since 1987, the River Project, a small environmental organization working from a Hudson River Pier a few blocks north of the World Trade Center in New York City, has been tracking the marine life in and around the pier areas of the Hudson River estuary. Almost 200 species have been found so far, including blue-fish, sturgeon, herring, shad, striped bass, lobsters, crabs, blowfish, and sea horses. The River Project sponsors environmental education programs and boating and fishing events and is working toward creating an "estuarium," which will display "the beautiful and exciting creatures that inhabit the still murky depths of the Hudson River estuary." Visitors are welcome at events and, by appointment, to view ongoing work.

◆ **FOR MORE INFORMATION:** The River Project, 67 Vestry Street, New York, NY 10013; 212-431-5787

Beach and Shore Walks

State and National Parks

New York and New Jersey beaches, meccas for sun wor-shippers, swimmers, and surfers during the summer months, are superb year-round walking environments. Several beaches, particu-larly those located in state or national recreation areas, have guided nature walks, hiking trails, and ranger-led interpretive programs. The wilderness area of the Fire Island National Seashore, the "walk-ing dunes" at Hither Hills State Park in Montauk, in New York State, and New Jersey's Island Beach and Cape May Point State Parks (see Chapter 3) offer diverse opportunities for littoral exploration.

◆ **FOR MORE INFORMATION:**

Fire Island National Seashore, 120 Laurel Street, Patchogue, NY 11772; 516-661-4876.

New York State Parks, Long Island Region, P.O. Box 247, Babylon, NY 11702; 516-669-1000.

Island Beach State Park, Seaside Park, NJ 08752; 908-793-0506.

Cape May Point State Park, P.O. Box 107, Cape May Point, NJ 08212; 609-884-5404.

Gateway National Recreation Area

The Gateway National Recreation Area, America's first urban national park, forms the entrance, or gateway, to New York Harbor with sites in both New York and New Jersey. Its 26,000 acres include trails through ocean and bay beaches in Brooklyn, Queens, and Staten Island, as well as the Jamaica Bay Wildlife Refuge and Sandy Hook (see Chapter 3). Park rangers lead several programs every weekend that explore this natural and recreational resource. These include nature walks, astronomy sessions, fishing lessons, beach and dune hikes, history walks, and nighttime explorations. Quarterly program guides are mailed free of charge.

◆ **FOR MORE INFORMATION:** Gateway National Recreation Area, Division of Interpretation and Recreation, Floyd Bennett Field, Brooklyn, NY 11234; 718-338-3338.

Horseshoe Crab Watches

The full moon in the month of May brings an incredible natural ritual to beaches up and down the New York and New Jersey coasts as thousands of horseshoe crabs, creatures that date back to dinosaur days, come ashore to mate and lay eggs by the hundreds of thousands. The egg laying coincides with the northern shorebird migration, when birds, making their first landfall since leaving South America, stop and eat the eggs, getting the protein they need for their own egg development. It's a spectacular sight, especially in the South Jersey and Delaware Bay areas, which attract the highest concentration of crabs and birds. Park rangers and groups, such as the American Littoral Society (see below), often lead special beach trips at this time of year.

American Littoral Society

With beach walks, fishing trips, conferences, nature cruises, shore clean-ups, and, when necessary, litigation, the American Littoral Society teaches and protects the beauty and value of the nation's shore areas. Headquartered at Sandy Hook, New Jersey, this national nonprofit organization leads an active program of field trips in New York and New Jersey. Recent events have included winter beach hikes, harbor seal walks, whale watches, canoe trips, overnight pelagic bird cruises, fish tagging, hawk watches, and members' parties. Membership: $25. There is a transportation/accommodations charge for trips.

◆ **FOR MORE INFORMATION:** American Littoral Society, Headquarters, Sandy Hook, Highlands, NJ 07732; 908-291-0055. New York Chapter, 28 West Ninth Road, Broad Channel, NY 11693; 718-634-6467.

The following groups also lead walks, camping trips, and other outings on Fire Island, Eastern Long Island, the New Jersey coast, and the Hudson and Delaware River shores:

Appalachian Mountain Club, 202 East 39th Street, New York, NY 10016; 212-986-1430.

Long Island Greenbelt Trail Conference, Inc., 23 Deep Path Road, Central Islip, NY 11722; 516-360-0753.

The Shorewalkers, Box 20748, Cathedral Station, New York, NY 10025; 212-330-7686.

Nature Preserves and Observatories

The Nature Conservancy

Founded in 1951, the Nature Conservancy is a nonprofit, 700,000-member national organization, with "a straightforward goal: to protect rare plants and animals by protecting the places they need to survive." It accomplishes its mission by purchasing threatened land and establishing nature preserves. There are 1,300 such preserves nationwide, including several in New York and New Jersey. The Mashomack Preserve on Shelter Island (see Chapter 3) is one of the largest. The Conservancy plays a major role in spearheading environmental projects and running nature programs on Long Island, including walks, photography workshops, and birdwatching excursions.

◆ **FOR MORE INFORMATION:** The Nature Conservancy, International Headquarters, 1815 North Lynn Street, Arlington, VA 22209; 703-841-5300.

Edwin B. Forsythe National Wildlife Refuge

Located in the tidal wetlands just north of Atlantic City, New Jersey, the Brigantine division of this National Wildlife Refuge is considered one of the top ten birding spots in the USA. The 20,000-square-acre sanctuary, established in 1929, is unusual because it has two large freshwater ponds, created by a system of dikes, within a large salt marsh area. The area is impressive for both the variety (300 species) and the sheer number of birds it attracts. During the fall migration, 100,000 birds, mostly snow geese and brant, often arrive at the same time, and about 50 percent of the Atlantic Coast black duck population winters in the area. Other times you'll see herons, egrets, ibises, geese, and small songbirds amidst the marsh grasses and wildflowers.

The refuge has two short walking trails, as well as an eight-mile self-guided tour that you can travel by car, bike, or on foot. You'll see the greatest variety of birds from March through May and September through November. (Insects dominate in the summer months.) Open year-round sunrise to sunset. Admission: $3 per vehicle.

In 1984, the U.S. Department of the Interior created the Edwin B. Forsythe National Wildlife Refuge by combining Brigantine with the refuge in the Barnegat region to the north. This area includes Holgate Beach, a remarkably unspoiled barrier beach at the tip of Long Beach Island, a principal nesting area for endangered birds such as the piping plover, least tern and black skimmer. The beach is closed from April to September to protect the habitat. But it is open the remainder of the year for beach walks, fishing, and nature study.

◆ **FOR MORE INFORMATION:** Edwin B. Forsythe National Wildlife Refuge, Great Creek Road, P.O. Box 72, Oceanville, NJ 08231; 609-652-1665.

The Wetlands Institute

The Wetlands Institute, located in Stone Harbor on New Jersey's Cape, unveils the mysteries and highlights the importance of wetland areas. Hands-on exhibits, a children's discovery room, an observation deck overlooking 6,000 acres of coastal wetlands, a guided salt marsh trail, special programs, and an introductory film are featured. Founded in 1969 by conservationist Herbert H. Mills, the privately supported, not-for-profit institute aims to "encourage understanding and appreciation of the unique value of coastal wetlands" and to provide opportunities for people to enjoy the natural coastal environment. The Wings 'n Water Festival, held annually on the third weekend in September, brings thousands to the institute for boat cruises, a carving show, wildlife arts and crafts, games, and food. Open year-round, crowded on rainy summer days. Admission: $3 adults; $1 children.

◆ **FOR MORE INFORMATION:** The Wetlands Institute, 1075 Stone Harbor Boulevard, Stone Harbor, NJ 08247; 609-368-1211

Bird-watching in Cape May

Cape May is the bird-watching capital of North America, according to the New Jersey Audubon Society, which runs the Cape May Bird Observatory. Its peninsular shape, diverse habitat, and location as the last point of land before Delaware Bay attract migrating birds by the hundreds of thousands every fall. A raised observation platform in Cape May Point State Park is a prime spot for watching, and observers keep a running tally of the number of hawks that pass by in September and October — usually between 40,000 and 60,000.

The observatory conducts research, maintains a birding hot line, and sponsors field trips and educational programs throughout the year, including a two-day "Birdwatching for Beginners" workshop for $15.

The Cape May Migratory Bird Refuge, a 187-acre wetland and beachfront area owned by the not-for-profit Nature Conservancy, is another Cape May birding resource. The refuge provides a protected nesting place for piping plovers and least terns and has a one-mile loop trail, which is open to the public for "careful day use," from dawn until dusk.

◆ **FOR MORE INFORMATION:**

New Jersey Audubon Society's Cape May Bird Observatory, P.O. Box 3, Cape May Point, NJ 08212; 609-884-2736.

Cape May Point State Park, P.O. Box 107, Cape May Point, NJ 08212; 609-884-2159.

Cape May Migratory Bird Refuge, The Nature Conservancy, 200 Pottersville Road, Chester, NJ 07930; 908-439-3007.

◆ 8 ◆
Waterside
Festivals and Events

From Montauk to Cape May, Delaware Bay to the Erie Canal, waterfront festivals and special events celebrate maritime traditions — both old and new — and provide ways for visitors to learn something new, get some exercise, eat food, and enjoy a day or an evening by the water. The following is a sampling of the shore walks, seafood festivals, boat parades, and special events held throughout New York and New Jersey. Since many of these events are volunteer-organized and subject to change, it's best to call ahead to confirm.

January

New York

Guided New Year's Day Beach Walk in Breezy Point, Queens. A naturalist discusses beach ecology during a free two-to-three-mile walk along the beach. Refreshments. A similar walk takes place the same day at Jones Beach. January 1, 11:00 a.m. American Littoral Society, 718-634-6467.

New York National Boat Show. Annual indoor boating spectacular at the Javits Convention Center in Manhattan. Hundreds of boats, from million-dollar cruisers to dinghies, and the latest equipment and gear are displayed. Boating lectures. Early January. Admission is charged. Javits Center, 212-216-2000.

New Jersey

Guided New Year's Day Beach Walk in Sandy Hook. A naturalist discusses beach ecology during a free two-to-three-mile walk along the beach. Refreshments. January 1, 11:00 a.m. American Littoral Society, 908-291-0055.

February

New York

Annual Boat Show at the Nassau Coliseum, Uniondale. New boats, accessories, and services. Displays include six-foot raft and fifty-foot yacht. Admission: $8 adults, children age ten and under, free. Tobay Beach Marina. Two weekends in February. New York Marine Trades Association, 516-691-7050.

New Jersey

Sail Expo, Atlantic City Convention Center. Annual nine-day sailors' get-together and show. Boat and equipment displays, over 300 seminars and lectures, dinners, parties, and an indoor sailing pool. American Sail Advancement Program, 401-841-0900.

Seal-A-Bration, New Jersey State Aquarium. Seal festival with educational displays, live seals, life-size eleven-foot model of an elephant seal, games, and children's activities. 1 Riverside Drive, Camden. Late February or early March. 609-365-3300.

April

New York

Walk Off the Lamb. Shorewalkers' annual post-Easter thirteen-mile ramble along Manhattan's Harlem and East Rivers from Inwood to South Street Seaport. Held the Saturday after Easter. 212-330-7686.

American Littoral Society Ecology Cruise from Sheepshead Bay, Brooklyn. Three-hour bird-watching cruise with information on natural and human history of Jamaica Bay. Admission: $25, including continental breakfast. Pier 6, Emmons Avenue and Dooley Street. American Littoral Society, 718-634-6467.

Heckscher Spring Festival, East Islip. Environmental displays, clowns, games, pony rides, photography exhibit, live entertainment. Free. Heckscher State Park. A weekend close to Earth Day. Long Island State Parks, 516-669-1000, ext. 247.

Hudson River Shadfests: Shad season begins with the first forsythia bloom, and towns along the Hudson celebrate with festivals featuring free tastes of baked, smoked, and potted shad. Music, entertainment, craft sales, and displays about river history and ecology add to the fun. Festivals coordinated by the Hudson River Foundation held weekends from late April through May in different Hudson River towns. Hudson River Foundation, 212-924-8290.

New Jersey

Somers Point Bayfest. This seafood festival offers environmental displays and crafts for sale. Municipal Beach, New Jersey Avenue and the Bay. Saturday of Earth Week. Somers Point Office of Community Education and Recreation, 609-927-5253.

Earth Day Celebration, New Jersey State Aquarium. Displays on protecting the earth and the ocean, entertainment. Participation by numerous environmental and wildlife protection organizations. 1 Riverside Drive, Camden. Weekend of Earth Week. 609-365-3300.

Ocean City DooDah Parade. Comic event to celebrate the end of tax season. Suitcase drill teams, pooper scooper brigades, clowns, pets in cars, Mummers and Hobo Band. Downtown. Late April. Ocean City Public Relations Office, 609-525-9300.

Lambertville Shad Festival. This two-day festival commemorates the arrival of shad as they swim upriver to spawn in the Delaware River. Arts and crafts. Many other river communities in New York and New Jersey hold shad festivals at this season, but this is the biggest. Bridge and Union Streets. Lambertville Chamber of Commerce, 609-397-0055.

May

New York

Fleet Week in New York Harbor. International naval review and celebration. Includes a ship parade, tours of visiting ships, military band concerts, crew canoe races, and athletic competitions. Events are on Hudson River and at the Intrepid Sea•Air•Space Museum, Manhattan. Held annually in May or June. Intrepid Museum, 212-245-2533.

Spring Launchings at South Street Seaport, Lower Manhattan. Annual seaport work day. Grubby work, good food, and festive atmosphere draw hundreds of volunteers to help the museum get its sailing vessels and waterfront ready for the season. First Saturday in May. 212-748-8600.

The Great Saunter. All day, thirty-two-mile shoreside walk around the island of Manhattan. Starts and ends at South Street Seaport. See Statue of Liberty, New Jersey Palisades, fishermen, blooming cherry trees, Little Red Lighthouse, parks, construction sites, cement plants, cruise liners, workboats. Convenient entry and drop-out points. Sponsored by the Shorewalkers. $10 donation for nonmembers. First weekend in May. 212-330-7686.

Shadfest and Opening Day Celebration at Hudson River Maritime Museum, Kingston. Music, crafts, food, shad dinners on the banks of historic Rondout Creek. Over 4,000 people attend this festival, which inaugurates the seasonal opening of the Hudson River Maritime Museum. 914-338-0071.

Harborfest Dock Day in Port Washington. Entertainment, boat rides, crafts, children's fun park, food, nautical demonstrations, and Enviro-Expo. Free. Town Dock. Saturday before Memorial Day weekend. Port Washington Chamber of Commerce, 516-883-6566.

Spring Rodeo Fishing Tournament at Jones Beach, Wantagh, Captree State Park in Islip, and Robert Moses State Park. Participants compete for largest of four species of fish by weight. Top prize is $250, with equipment prizes for other winners. Entry fee: $5. Saturday and Sunday in mid-May. Long Island State Parks, 516-669-1000, ext. 247.

New Jersey

Ocean City Spring Festival. Mile-long event with more than 450 crafters and displays. Includes entertainment and Greek Food Festival. Downtown from 6th to 14th Streets on Asbury Avenue. Early May. Ocean City Public Relations Office, 609-525-9300.

Ocean City Annual Martin Z. Mollusk Day. Hermit crab attempts to see her/his shadow. Gala celebration. Moorlyn Terrace Beach between 8th and 9th Streets. Early May. Ocean City Public Relations Office, 609-525-9300.

Annual Manasquan River Canoe Race, Howell. Eight-mile race for beginners and experienced paddlers. Howell Park Golf Course, Preventorium Road. Hours: 8:00 a.m. to 4:30 p.m. Entry fee: $12.50 per person. Monmouth County Parks Department, 908-842-4000.

Stone Harbor Boat Show. Boats, cars, food, music, and family entertainment. 96th Street and the Beach. Mother's Day weekend. Stone Harbor Chamber of Commerce, 609-368-6101.

American Littoral Society Cape May Birdwatching Expedition. Annual outing along shores of the Delaware Bay in Cape May County to witness spring shorebird migration. Admission: $10 plus annual membership, which is $25 for adults, $15 for students and seniors. Meet at Jake's Landing. Mid-May. American Littoral Society, 908-291-0055.

Summer

New York

Fulton Fish Market Tour, Lower Manhattan. Early morning, behind-the-scenes tours of the historic, still frantically busy market with educator M. J. Shaughnessy. Admission: $10. Spring through fall. South Street Seaport Museum, 212-748-8600.

Intrepid Museum Seafest. Season-long series of ship visits and pier events at the Intrepid Sea•Air•Space Museum on the Hudson River in Manhattan. Visiting vessels include police, fire, and pilot boats, and the "sunken-ship" *Frying Pan*. Summer weekends. 212-245-2533.

Jones Beach Summer Concert Series. Top-name jazz and rock artists appear at Jones Beach Theater. Admission: $30 and up, depending on bill of fare. June through September, mostly on weekends. Long Island State Parks, 516-669-1000, ext. 247.

Long Island Summer Cultural Arts Concert Series. Many different types of music at various parks. July through September. Long Island State Parks, 516-669-1000, ext. 247.

Long Beach Summer Concert Series. Country, ethnic, big band, banjo, and easy listening music three times a week at three or four locations along the Boardwalk. Free. City of Long Beach Department of Recreation, 516-431-3890.

Harrison Street Regatta, Lower Manhattan. Held — when tide and time suit the organizers — every summer since 1980, this

Fulton Fish Market

is one of New York Harbor's most offbeat and fascinating on-the-water spectacles. Participants battle tricky river currents and race human-powered watercraft (no sails or engines allowed) from a Lower Manhattan pier to New Jersey and back. The second-place finisher wins, which makes for often-hilarious maneuvering. Spectators and participants welcome. Downtown Boat Club, 212-966-1852.

New Jersey

Laser Light Show, Point Pleasant Beach. Free laser light extravaganza every Sunday evening in July and August. Jenkinson's Beach, Parkway and Ocean Avenue. Jenkinson's Pavilion, 908-899-0569.

Jenkinson's Fireworks, Point Pleasant Beach. Fireworks display every Thursday evening in July and August. Jenkinson's Beach, Parkway and Ocean Avenue. Jenkinson's Pavilion, 908-899-0569.

Children's Beach Shows. Various free live shows for kids every Monday in July and August. Jenkinson's Beach, Parkway and Ocean Avenue, Point Pleasant. Jenkinson's Pavilion, 908-899-0569.

Festival of the Atlantic, Point Pleasant Beach. Forty-two-member symphony orchestra performs eight free Wednesday evening concerts on the beach. Jenkinson's North at the Inlet, Ocean Avenue and Broadway. Jenkinson's Pavilion, 908-899-0569.

Ocean City Pops Concert Series. Varied popular and classical concerts by Ocean City's all-professional orchestra-in-residence. Gala Opening usually free. Performances several days a week in July, August, and September. Admission: $3 to $10, depending on the program. Music Pier, Boardwalk and Moorlyn Terrace. Ocean City Public Relations Office, 609-525-9300.

Somers Point Concert on the Beach Series. Free concerts every Friday, featuring a wide variety of music, including rock, jazz, country, reggae, and more. Municipal Beach, Bay and New Jersey Avenues. Early July through week after Labor Day. Somers Point Community Education and Recreation Office, 609-927-5253.

Pepsi Fireworks Spectacular, Seaside Heights. Fireworks display every Wednesday evening. Hamilton Avenue and Boardwalk. Early July through mid-September. Seaside Business Association, 800-SEA-SHOR.

Alliance for a Living Ocean Eco-Tour of Long Beach Island, Ship Bottom. Trolley tour includes hands-on activities to discover barrier island environmental systems and how to preserve them. Two different three-hour tours offered weekly on different days. Child- and adult-oriented information packets come with tour. Admission: $10 (kids five and under are free). Chamber of Commerce Building, 265 West 9th Street. July and August. Alliance for a Living Ocean, 609-492-0222.

Sea Isle City Beachcomber Walks. Conducted by the Sea Isle City Environmental Commission, these award-winning walks provide little-known information about sea creatures and the marine environment with an emphasis on ecological awareness. Beachcombing begins after brief presentation and ends with an explanation of what group members have found. 29th Street Beach (bulletin board at this location describes a self-guided walk, with information on seashells and the environment). Tuesdays and Thursdays at 10:00 a.m., mid-June through Labor Day. Sea Isle City group has trained guides in Ocean City and Cape May for similar walks. For information: Sea Isle City Tourism Office, 609-263-TOUR.

Long Beach Island Museum Walking Tours, Beach Haven. Guided tours of local historic homes and bed and breakfasts leave museum every Tuesday and Friday at 10:30 a.m. Engleside and Beach Avenues. Admission: $3. End of June through the week after Labor Day. Long Beach Island Museum, 609-492-0700.

Captain Ocean's Environmental Series, Wildwood. Local merchants dip a net in the ocean and describe whatever they catch, then put living organisms back in the water. Mondays at Rambler Road and the Beach, Thursdays between Spicer and Spencer Avenues at the Beach. Free. 609-522-1407.

Salt Marsh Safaris. Guided eco-tours of Stone Harbor area wetlands. Mondays through Saturdays at 10:00 a.m., noon, and 2:00 p.m. Sundays at 11:00 a.m. and 1:00 p.m. Admission: $4 adults; $2 children. 1075 Stone Harbor Boulevard. Wetlands Institute, 609-368-1211.

June

New York

Clearwater's Great Hudson River Revival. Two-day celebration of river traditions with top-name musical entertainment — folk, jazz, blues, gospel, old-time — appearing on seven stages. Storytelling, dancing, mimes, crafts, food, special programs for kids. Headliners in 1994 included Tom Paxton, Sweet Honey in the Rock, Raffi, Pete Seeger. Held every June at Westchester County Community College, Valhalla. Tickets: $20/day; $28/weekend. Discounts available. Clearwater, 914-454-7673.

Blessing of the Fleet in Montauk. Decorated boats parade out of Lake Montauk into Montauk Harbor for blessing by a Protestant pastor, a Catholic priest, and a Jewish rabbi. Followed by memorial service for those lost at sea. Montauk Chamber of Commerce, 516-668-2428.

Harbor and Carousel Festival, Rochester. This ten-day mega-festival, from the Erie Canal via the Genesee River to the shore of Lake Ontario, features a boat parade, sand sculpturing, and a volley ball tournament on the beach. Also: free lighthouse tours, free rides on a historic 1905 carousel, live entertainment, and more.

Ontario Beach Park. Early June. Greater Rochester Visitor's Association, 716-546-3070.

New Jersey

Delaware Bay Day. Outdoor festival celebrating culture, history, traditional industries, and natural resources of the bay. Street and boat parades, food, crafts, music, hands-on exhibits, river tours, and fireworks. Sponsored by the Delaware Bay Schooner Project and held in the Maurice River towns of Bivalve, Shellpile, and Port Norris. Usually first weekend in June. 609-785-2060.

Kids' Fish 'n Krab Kontest, Barnegat. Contestants aged five to ten compete in two age groupings to catch the largest fish and largest crab. Prizes. Barnegat Boat Dock Parking Area, Barnegat Bay and Bayshore Drive. Usually in June. 609-698-8526.

Annual New Jersey Fresh Seafood Festival, Atlantic City. Educational exhibits on marine topics, tall ships, rides, games, arts and crafts, entertainment and—of course—seafood (landlubber fare also available). Sponsored by a nonprofit organization, the two-day

Miss Crustacean Hermit Crab

festival donates all proceeds to ecological and scientific groups promoting ocean awareness. Gardner's Basin, Maritime Park, 800 North New Hampshire Avenue. Second weekend in June. New Jersey Fresh Seafood Festival, Inc., 609-FISH-FUN.

New Jersey Seafood Festival, Belmar. Two-day event with food, entertainment, arts and crafts, educational exhibits, and children's activities. Silver Lake Park, Fifth and Ocean Avenues. Belmar Chamber of Commerce, 908-681-2900.

July

New York

Long Beach Summer Arts and Crafts Festival. On the Boardwalk at Riverside Boulevard. Free admission. The weekend after July 4. Long Beach Recreation Department, 516-431-3890.

Hudson River Maritime Museum Tugboat Day, Kingston. Historic tugs gather in Rondout Creek. Tugboat tours and rides, music, crafts, food. Held on Saturday during summer, 914-338-0071.

Medina Canal Festival. Hometown celebration in one of the Erie Canal's larger posts. Parades, fireworks, entertainment. Medina Canal Festival Committee, 716-798-0889.

Tonawanda CanalFest. Week-long event offers concessions, food, bands and other entertainment, a water ski show, boat parades and model boats, children's events. Weekend performances by Buffalo Philharmonic Orchestra and Empire State Ballet. Third week in July. Tonawanda Chamber of Commerce, 716-692-5120.

New Jersey

Bell Atlantic Sandcastle Contest, Belmar. Competition for all ages with prizes. Attracts thousands. Fifth Avenue Beach. Belmar Chamber of Commerce, 908-681-2900.

Wooden Boat Festival, Toms River. Sail race featuring such rare boats as Sneak Boxes and A Cats. Entire race can be seen from dock. Wooden boat displays, maritime craft vendors, and family fun. Toms River Yacht Club, Riviera Drive. Third Sunday in July. Toms River Seaport Society, 609-845-0717.

Ocean City Night in Venice Boat Parade and Bay Celebration. More than one hundred decorated boats sail in and out of city lagoons. Decorated bay-front homes. Great Egg Harbor Bay, Inland Waterway from Longport Bridge to 23rd Street. Date and other information: Ocean City Public Relations Office, 609-525-9300.

Baymen's Festival, Tuckerton. This celebration of baymen's traditions offers exhibits and demonstrations of such crafts as boat-building and decoy carving. Admission: $15, which includes a visit to the Barnegat Bay Decoy and Baymen's Museum and an all-you-can-eat pig roast and seafood dinner. Mid-July. Barnegat Bay Decoy and Baymen's Museum, 609-296-8868.

August

New York

New Ship and Boat Model Festival, South Street Seaport Museum, Lower Manhattan. Builders display their model boats, demonstrate skills and techniques, and discuss approaches to this folk art. Model boat building workshop for children. Pier 16. First weekend in August. South Street Seaport Museum, 212-748-8600.

Antique and Classic Boat Show, Hudson River Maritime Museum, Kingston. Thirty-five to forty antique boats, from cruisers to runabouts, gather for public viewing. Arts and crafts exhibits, including scrimshaw, model boat displays, maritime paintings and drawings. Music, food. 914-338-0071.

Annual Paumanauke Pow Wow, Copiague. Native Americans from tribes nationwide exhibit and demonstrate their art, crafts, and beadwork. Native American food, jewelry, dance competitions, and drumming. Tanner Park. Second weekend in August. Babylon Citizen's Council on the Arts, 516-661-7558.

Long Beach Summer Arts and Crafts Festival. On the Boardwalk at Riverside Boulevard. Free admission. Second weekend in August. Long Beach Recreation Department, 516-431-3890.

Fire Island Lighthouse Barefoot Black Tie Gala. Festive fundraiser for the continued preservation of the Fire Island Lighthouse. Guests are required to wear at least one item of formal attire (boxer shorts with a black tie, for example, will pass muster). Food, drinks, dancing in tents near the lighthouse beach. Parking available. Admission: about $40, including dinner. Fire Island Lighthouse Preservation Society, 516-321-7028.

Little Falls Canal Days. Three-day event at three sites, with free buses from one location to another. Continuous music by a variety of bands plus other entertainment. The tugboat *Urger* docks in town for the event. Crafts fair, juried art show, car show, races, wine tasting, pig roast, and other food. Little Falls YMCA, 315-823-1740.

New Jersey

Ocean City Miss Crustacean Hermit Crab Beauty Pageant and Crab Races. Billed as world's only hermit crab beauty pageant, including races and prizes. Preliminary to Weird Contest Week later in the month, with french fry and saltwater taffy sculpting, artistic pie eating, wet T-shirt tossing, and animal impersonations. Beach at 6th Street. Early August. Ocean City Public Relations Office, 609-525-9300.

Barnegat Lighthouse Historical Slide Show. Outdoor slide show with music on history of Barnegat Lighthouse and Long Beach Island from Native American times to present. Donation. Barnegat Lighthouse State Park. First Sunday in August at sunset. Barnegat Light Borough Hall, 609-494-9196.

Sea Shanty Festival, New Jersey State Aquarium. Sea shanty singing and folk dancing. 1 Riverside Drive, Camden. Two weekends before Labor Day. 609-365-3300.

Harborfest at Historic Gardner's Basin, Atlantic City. Attractions include New Jersey Symphony Orchestra, World Championship Ocean Marathon Swim, replicas of Roaring Twenties rum-running vessels, and Prohibition era–style speakeasies. Also: food, live music, rides and midway amusements, arts and crafts displays. North New Hampshire Avenue and the Bay. Historic Gardner's Basin, 609-348-2880.

Annual Long Beach Island Lifeguard Tournament, Beach Haven. Beach patrols on Long Beach Island demonstrate ocean rescue skills in competitive events. Ocean Beach, 110th Street. Mid-August. 609-361-1200.

Sea Isle City Festival by the Bay. This evening event features an old-timers' demonstration of such skills as net mending and fish cleaning. Seafood, environmental displays, children's activities. 42nd Street and the Bay. Late August. Sea Isle City Tourism Office, 609-236-TOUR.

Autumn

New York

Marine Sciences Research Center Open House, State University of New York, Stony Brook. Environmental and other scientific displays, marine videos, programming for children on local marine ecology. 516-632-8700.

American Littoral Society Ecology Cruise from Sheepshead Bay, Brooklyn. Three-hour bird-watching cruise with information on the natural and human history of Jamaica Bay. Admission: $25, including continental breakfast. Pier 6, Emmons Avenue and Dooley Street. 718-634-6467.

September

New York

In-Water Boat Show, South Street Seaport, Lower Manhattan. Powerboats, sailboats, accessories, and services. Admission: $6 adults; $3 children twelve and under. Pier 16 and special floating docks. South Street Seaport Museum, 212-748-8600.

Annual New York Wooden Boat Festival at South Street Seaport, Lower Manhattan. Builders exhibit and sell handcrafted kayaks, skiffs, canoes, and runabouts. Demonstrations of boatbuilding techniques, wood carving, and the making of models, scrimshaw, rigging, and fancy rope work. Free admission. Pier 16. 212-748-8600.

Annual Mayor's Cup Race, South Street Seaport, Lower Manhattan. Part of the Wooden Boat Classic Regatta Series held annually in the Northeast to celebrate the tradition of offshore and coastal fishing vessels racing back to port with their catches. Competition for classic schooners, sloops, cutters, ketches, and yawls built or designed before 1960. For an unobstructed view, onlookers can book space on the Seaport Liberty Cruises spectators' boat. Boat tickets: $20. 212-748-8600.

Intrepid Tugboat Challenge, Manhattan. New York Harbor tugs compete to show their speed, power, and crew prowess in a boat race, nose-to-nose pushing contest, and crew line-heaving competition. Sponsored and hosted by the Intrepid Sea•Air•Space Museum. Spectators welcome. 212-245-2533.

Harvest Moon Festival, Hudson River Maritime Museum, Kingston. Celebration of Hudson River Valley agriculture. Hudson River Sloop *Clearwater* visits. Music, food, environmental displays. 914-338-0071.

Annual Festival by the Sea at Town Park, Lido Beach. The Town of Hempstead celebrates Long Island's maritime industry. Sailboat regatta, Coast Guard rescue display, surf casting, nautical merchandise vendors, run and swim biathlon, clowns, music, and seafood. Third weekend in September. Town of Hempstead, 516-489-5000, ext. 3440.

Sag Harbor Harborfest. Celebration of Sag Harbor's history as a whaling port. Whaleboat races, walking tours. Sag Harbor Chamber of Commerce, 516-725-0011.

Canaltown Days in Palmyra. Two-day event features horse-drawn parade, crafts, flea market, antiques, an art show, entertainment, and food. 315-597-2302.

Montauk Striped Bass Surf Fishing Tournament. Top prize $500, with equipment prizes for other winners. Entry fee: $5. Friday through Sunday at end of September. Long Island State Parks, 516-669-1000, ext. 247.

Captree Carnival at Captree State Park, Islip. U.S. Coast Guard hele-hoist rescue demonstration, scuba diving, fish filleting demo, nautical displays, crab races, clam shucking contest, raffles, kid's games and shows, free boat rides, food galore. Admission: free. Weekend in mid-September. Long Island State Parks, 516-669-1000, ext. 247.

Mt. Sinai Harborfest, Cedar Beach. One-day event features blues festival, whaleboat racing, arts and crafts, kite-flying contest, sports and dance demonstrations, amusements, games, and seafood. End of September or beginning of October. Miller Place/Mt. Sinai Chamber of Commerce, 516-821-1313.

Greenport Maritime Festival. Tall ships, wooden boat regatta, clam shucking and clam chowder contests, whaleboat race, visits by U.S. Coast Guard and U.S. Navy ships, sailboat rides to Bug Lighthouse, harbor tours, demonstrations of marine skills, exhibits at local museums, seafood, and more. Last weekend in September. East End Seaport and Maritime Museum, 516-477-0004.

Annual In-Water and On-Land Boat Show, Tobay Beach. New boats, accessories, and services. Displays include six-foot raft and fifty-foot yacht. Admission: $8 adults; children age ten and under free. Tobay Beach Marina. Last weekend in September and first weekend in October. New York Marine Trades Association, 516-691-7050.

New Jersey

Sandy Hook Shore Heritage Festival. Two-day celebration of the music, crafts, food, and history of Sandy Hook and the New Jersey Shore. Parade Ground, Historic Fort Hancock. Weekend after Labor Day. Gateway National Recreation Area, Sandy Hook Unit Visitors Center, 908-872-0115, ext. 217.

Jersey Shore Sea Kayaking and Bay Canoeing Show, Bayville. Bay canoeing, beginners clinics, displays and demonstrations, nature cruises, contests, and a kayak rolling clinic. Berkeley Island County Park, Brennin Concourse. Ocean County Department of Parks and Recreation, 609-971-3085.

In-Water Power Boat Show, Atlantic City. Hundreds of boats on display. Food, boat-related equipment vendors. Senator Frank S. Farley State Marina, 600 Huron Avenue. Four-day event, Thursday through Sunday of Labor Day weekend. Management Group, Inc., 609-441-8483.

Annual Wings 'n Water Festival in Stone Harbor, Avalon, and Middle Township. Three-day celebration of the New Jersey Coast begins Friday evening with benefit cocktail party and auction for Stone Harbor's Wetlands Institute. Wildlife arts and crafts, boat cruises, children's art and nature games, a carving show, model boats, environmental displays, a retriever demonstration, and food. A jitney transports participants among sites. Wetlands Institute, 609-368-1211.

Old Time Barnegat Bay Decoy and Gunning Show, Tuckerton. Exhibits and demonstrations of old and new decoys, boatbuilding, retriever contest, duck and goose calling, and music. Last full weekend in September. Ocean County Parks and Recreation Department, 609-971-3085.

Keyport Festival and Boat Races. Two-day weekend event includes food festival, boat races, pumpkin painting, children's activities, rides, and a classic and antique car show. Keyport Chamber of Commerce, 908-264-3626.

October

New York

Pumpkin Sail/Sale. Hudson River Sloop *Clearwater* sails down the Hudson with a cargo of pumpkins and music makers. Weekend river festivals in towns along the river include concerts, pumpkin sales, food, and crafts. 914-454-7673.

Long Island Seafood, Wine and Harborfest, Huntington. Tall ships, wine tasting, food festival, parade, five-kilometer run, arts and crafts, antique car show, and continuous live entertainment. First weekend in October. Huntington Chamber of Commerce, 516-423-6100.

Cold Spring Harbor Fish Hatchery Fall Fair. Food, turtles, child-oriented games, fishing for youngsters, displays by an array of environmental groups. Second Saturday in October. Cold Spring Harbor Fish Hatchery, 516-692-6868.

Great Long Island Duck Race, Dowling College, Oakdale. This benefit for Big Brothers and Big Sisters of Long Island takes place on the Connetquot River. Plastic ducks are numbered, adopted for $5 each by participants, and released into the river. Propelled by wind, current, and—if necessary—a fan, they "race" to a watery finish line. Adopter of the winning duck receives a $10,000 savings bond. The 3:30 p.m. race is preceded by a festival, beginning at 11:00 a.m., featuring children's theater, storytelling, crafts, circus workshops, magic, puppets, pony and carnival rides, pumpkin carving, and games. A Sunday in the first half of October. Big Brothers and Big Sisters of Long Island, 516-586-4715.

Fall and Apple Festivals, Sayville. Sayville Apple Festival falls on the same weekend as the three-day Discover Sayville Fall Festival, featuring face painting, entertainment, a pet parade, and hay and pony rides. The town was voted "friendliest in America" in a 1994 Newsday poll. Mid-October. Fall Festival information: Sayville Chamber of Commerce, 516-567-5257. Apple Festival information: Township of Islip, 516-224-5490.

Montauk Chamber of Commerce Fall Festival. Three-day event includes clam-chowder-tasting competition. Local restaurants submit chowder, and the public votes. Cost to tasters: $5 a mug for chowder and a refill. Other attractions: hay and pony rides, plant and yard sales, balloons, pumpkin decorating, live music, wine tasting, and a clam-shucking contest that draws some of the fastest shuckers on the East Coast. Columbus Day weekend. Montauk Chamber of Commerce, 516-668-2428.

Annual Oyster Festival on the streets of Oyster Bay. Oyster-shucking and -eating contests. (Eating record as of 1994: 244 oysters in two minutes, forty seconds.) Huge street fair, antique boats, harbor tours on the paddle-boat steamer *Thomas Jefferson*, food festival, juried crafts show, entertainment, five-kilometer run, and amateur and Olympic-quality professional cycling classic.

Weekend after Columbus Day. Oyster Bay Chamber of Commerce, 516-624-8082.

South Shore Fishing Classic at Captree State Park, Islip. Participants compete for largest striped bass or bluefish by weight. Fishing allowed from beach, surf, jetty, bank, or pier. Top prize $500, with equipment prizes for other winners. Entry fee: $5. Friday through Sunday in mid-October. Long Island State Parks, 516-669-1000, ext. 247.

South Street Seaport Museum and Marketplace Harvest Festival, Lower Manhattan. Kids of all ages decorate pumpkins, listen to spooky stories, and make masks. 207 Front Street. Late October. South Street Seaport Museum, 212-748-8600.

New Jersey

Chowderfest Weekend in Beach Haven. All-you-can-eat chowder cook-off, with some twenty-five Long Beach Island restaurants participating. Merchants Mart, country music, and more food. Admission: $6 for adults. Bayfront Park, Taylor Avenue. 800-292-6372 or Long Beach Island Chamber of Commerce, 609-494-7211.

Ocean City Indian Summer Block Party. Huge craft and seafood bazaar. Boardwalk and 5th to 14th Streets on Asbury Avenue. Columbus Day weekend. Ocean City Public Relations Office, 609-525-9300.

Annual Canoe Race in Toms River. Eight-mile race attracts entries in twelve categories. Entry fee. Meet at Old Toms River Bus Terminal, Iron Street. Transportation provided for participants and canoes to race starting point at River View. Ocean County Department of Parks and Recreation, 609-971-3085.

November

New York

Long Beach Youth Turkey Trot. Two-mile race for first-through twelfth-grade boys and girls. Winners get turkeys. Entry fee: $2. On the Boardwalk at Riverside Boulevard. Usually the weekend before Thanksgiving. Long Beach Department of Recreation, 516-431-3890.

Walk-Off-The-Turkey. Shorewalkers' annual thirteen-mile hike along the Hudson River in Manhattan from South Ferry to the Little Red Lighthouse beneath the George Washington Bridge. Held the Saturday after Thanksgiving. $5 donation suggested for nonmembers. 212-330-7686.

Long Island Environmental Expo, Melville. Exhibits and seminars aimed at businesses, but many of interest to environmentally conscious consumers. Displays by environmental and wildlife groups, including some with live animals and birds. Discussions on environmentally safe products and environmental protection, including the marine environment. Admission: free. Hauppauge Industrial Association, 516-543-5355.

New Jersey

Sea Story Festival, New Jersey State Aquarium. Story-telling, authors, and family entertainment to celebrate National Children's Book Week. 1 Riverside Drive, Camden. 609-365-3300.

Holiday Hoopla, Stone Harbor. Handmade environmental and other gifts, children's craft lessons, miniature trains, Christmas music, baked goods, and Santa. 1075 Stone Harbor Boulevard. Saturday after Thanksgiving. Wetlands Institute, 609-368-1211.

December

New York

Christmas at the Lighthouse. Rondout II Lighthouse, Kingston, is decorated for the holiday season, as it was when families lived there. Boats depart from the Hudson River Maritime Museum (weather permitting) for lighthouse tours. 914-338-0071.

New Jersey

Fort Hancock Historic Christmas, Sandy Hook. History House, a restored officer's home from the 1890s, is decorated each year in the style of a different historic period. Music and refreshments. Free. Mid-December. Gateway National Recreation Area Sandy Hook Unit Visitors Center, 908-872-0115, ext. 217.

Washington Crossing the Delaware, from Washington Crossing, Pennsylvania, to Titusville, New Jersey. In annual reenactment, Washington greets, reviews, and addresses his troops at McConkey's Inn on the Pennsylvania side, after which the players march to the visitors center of Pennsylvania's Washington Crossing State Park and cross the river to the park's New Jersey side for a brief greeting ceremony. Viewing sites in both states. Christmas Day at 1:00 p.m. Pennsylvania Washington Crossing State Park, 215-493-4076.

Index

182 ◆ New York and New Jersey Coastal Adventures

You just enjoyed a book from Country Roads Press; you'll be glad to know we also offer the following guide books, and we're adding new titles every season. If you're looking for a title not on the list, call us at the number below.

In the Country Roads series:
Country Roads of Alabama
Country Roads of Connecticut and Rhode Island
Country Roads of Florida
Country Roads of Georgia
Country Roads of Hawaii
Country Roads of Idaho
Country Roads of Illinois, 3rd ed.
Country Roads of Indiana
Country Roads of Iowa
Country Roads of Kentucky
Country Roads of Louisiana
Country Roads of Maine
Country Roads of Maryland and Delaware
Country Roads of Massachusetts, 2nd ed.
Country Roads of Michigan, 2nd ed.
Country Roads of Minnesota
Country Roads of Missouri
Country Roads of New York
Country Days In New York City
Country Roads of New Jersey
Country Roads of New Hampshire, 2nd ed.
Country Roads of North Carolina
Country Roads of Ohio
Country Roads of Ontario
Country Roads of Oregon
Country Roads of Pennsylvania
Country Roads of Southern California
Country Roads of Tennessee
Country Roads of Texas
Country Roads of the Maritimes
Country Roads of Vermont
Country Roads of Virginia
Country Roads of Washington

In the Country Towns series:
Country Towns of Arkansas
Country Towns of Florida
Country Towns of Georgia
Country Towns of Michigan
Country Towns of New York
Country Towns of Northern California

Country Towns of Pennsylvania
Country Towns of Southern California
Country Towns of Texas
Country Towns of Vermont

In the 52 Weekends series:
52 Florida Weekends $12.95
52 Illinois Weekends
52 Indiana Weekends $12.95
52 Michigan Weekends
52 New Jersey Weekends $12.95
52 New York Weekends
52 Northern California Weekends $12.95
52 Virginia Weekends $12.95
52 Wisconsin Weekends

In the Natural Wonders series:
Green Guide to Hawaii
Natural Wonders of Alaska
Natural Wonders of Connecticut & Rhode Island
Natural Wonders of Florida
Natural Wonders of Georgia $12.95
Natural Wonders of Idaho
Natural Wonders of Maine
Natural Wonders of Massachusetts
Natural Wonders of Michigan
Natural Wonders of New Mexico $12.95
Natural Wonders of New Hampshire
Natural Wonders of New Jersey
Natural Wonders of New York
Natural Wonders of Northern California $12.95
Natural Wonders of Ohio
Natural Wonders of Oregon $12.95
Natural Wonders of Southern California
Natural Wonders of Texas
Natural Wonders of Vermont $12.95
Natural Wonders of Virginia
Natural Wonders of Washington $12.95
Natural Wonders of Wisconsin

Along the Shore:
California Under Sail
Florida Under Sail
New England Under Sail $12.95
Maine: Cruising the Coast by Car
New York–New Jersey Coastal Adventures

Unless otherwise indicated, all books are $9.95 at bookstores.
Or order directly from the publisher; we're happy to take your request.
(Add $3.00 shipping and handling for direct orders.):
Country Roads Press
P.O. Box 286
Castine, Maine 04421
Toll-free phone number: **800-729-9179**